GARTH TURNER'S

2000

RRSP

GUIDE

Other books by Garth Turner

2020: New Rules for the New Age
2015: After the Boom
The Strategy: A Homeowner's Guide to Wealth Creation
The Defence: Guarding Your Money in Uncertain Times

GARTH TURNER'S

2000 RRSP GUIDE

HOW TO BUILD YOUR WEALTH AND **RETIRE IN COMFORT**

KEY PORTER BOOKS

Canadian Cataloguing in Publication Data
RRSP guide

Annual.
2000-
Continues: Turner, Garth. Garth Turner's RRSP guide ; ISSN 1482-003X
Important information for your RRSP contribution.
ISSN: 1490-2257
ISBN: 1-55263-106-0 (2000 issue)

1. Registered Retirement Savings Plans – Periodicals. 2. Tax shelters – Canada – Periodicals.
I. Title. II. Title: Retirement guide.

HD7129.T87 332.6′042 C99-900791-2

THE CANADA COUNCIL FOR THE ARTS SINCE 1957 | LE CONSEIL DES ARTS DU CANADA DEPUIS 1957

The publisher gratefully acknowledges the support of the Canada Council for the Arts and the Ontario Arts Council for its publishing program.

Canada

We acknowledge the financial support of the Government of Canada through the Book Publishing Industry Development Program (BPIDP) for our publishing activities.

Key Porter Books Limited
70 The Esplanade
Toronto, Ontario
Canada M5E 1R2

www.keyporter.com

Credits: Pp. 12, 26, 50, 143, reprinted with permission from *The Globe and Mail.*
Electronic formatting: Heidi Palfrey

Printed and bound in Canada

99 00 01 02 03 6 5 4 3 2 1

Contents

Introduction

Well, here we are, through the door of a brand-new century and a new millennium. What better time in your life to take stock of where you are, and where you are going in terms of your finances? If you are in your twenties, just starting out, then this is an ideal time to set a goal and make the bustling economy of the next decade work for you.

If you are a baby boomer like me, then you are just entering the most critical 10 years in terms of getting ready for what could be a very long and very pleasant retirement, if you make the right choices. And if you are close to retirement, or facing the conversion of your RRSP to a RRIF, then there are definitely things you need to know about right now.

This *2000 RRSP Guide* is designed to help you at all these critical stages of life. It gives you lots of strategies to employ, from the most cautious and conservative to the more aggressive. You will find checklists of things to do and actions to avoid. It will show you how, and why, to get 100% foreign content in your RRSP, and even how to exceed the government's stated RRSP contribution limits. It will demonstrate how your retirement plans and your home can intersect and how to make regular RRSP contributions even when you do not have extra cash.

But this book aims to go beyond the "how-to" part of retirement planning. I also want to give you a context within which to take action.

And that's where the Vision Thing comes in.

THE MISTAKES WE ARE MAKING

The greatest mistake Canadians make when it comes to their finances is being too timid and fearful. There was no better example of this than what happened in 1999. Following a violent but temporary correction on global financial markets in the fall of 1998 (which I flagged for you last year as the giant buying opportunity it turned out to be), many investors lost their nerve in the wake of market volatility and poor-performing mutual funds.

New sales of funds during all of 1999 were dismal—about half the levels of a year before. Meanwhile a lot of new money went into places perceived as safer, like money market funds, GICs, Canada Savings Bonds, and segregated funds. Part of the reason for this was Y2K anxiety, despite the fact that every major bank, Canadian corporation, utility, and government said it was ready for the new millennium.

Some fears were stoked by media commentators, authors, and financial advisers who insisted that financial Armageddon was at hand and who were, in my view, irresponsible alarmists who cared more about selling books and newsletters than helping people. But they succeeded in frightening people into making the wrong investments—at least, wrong in my view.

Why wrong? Because while people were busy hiding their money from perceived risk, the following were taking place:

- A dramatic recovery in Asian economies with increasing consumer confidence, industrial production, and rising markets. Asian and Japanese stocks and mutual funds soared in value.
- A technological revolution with a huge increase in the penetration of the Internet and a corresponding leap higher by science and technology funds and the Nasdaq.
- Many record new highs posted by the Dow Jones Industrials as that index sped through the 11,000 mark after being at 7500 in the fall of 1998.
- In the first nine months of 1999 the average gain recorded by the 10 top-performing Canadian mutual funds was an eye-popping 136%.

- In that same period more than 550 Canadian funds posted annual gains of 10%, and 330 gave investors a yield of more than 15%.

Of course, people who retreated into the safety of cash or fixed-income investments missed all of that and, if the statistics are correct, most of us cannot afford to lose any time at all. Canada's aging population poses a serious threat in decades to come, as I will elaborate on in Chapter 2. By 2015 half the population will be over the age of 40, for the first time ever. By 2030 there will be 140% more retired people than today and 8 million 70-year-olds. That will put a huge strain on the health care system and could bankrupt the Canada Pension Plan, despite recent attempts to save it. This will not be good news to that majority of Canadians who will retire over the next 20 years without any corporate pension whatsoever.

Today the average RRSP contains just $37,000, and the average contribution is just $4000. At this rate today's 50-year-old baby boomer will have accumulated less than $100,000 by age 65—about 10% of what will actually be needed.

But, the situation is far worse than even that suggests, because in 1999 two-thirds of all people eligible to make an RRSP contribution did not! Just one in 10 made the maximum contribution. So, clearly, we are falling behind. More people need to know the rules, the power of an RRSP, and just how easy it is to grow sheltered money while cutting your income tax bill. Clearly, with a retirement crisis brewing, making the most of today's booming economy is paramount.

NOW FOR THE GOOD NEWS

There is a silver lining to this retirement storm cloud, however. It's this: The next decade or more will likely offer some fabulous opportunities for long-term RRSP investors. There are many reasons to be optimistic, and to believe in economic growth and soaring stock and mutual fund values, including:

- The end of inflation as we know it. Many prices will be falling, instead of rising, increasing the disposable income people have available for investment.
- Stable or declining interest rates, which will lower the costs of mortgages and car leases along with corporate overhead, helping financial markets to rise.

Source: Raeside, Toronto Star

- Government budget surpluses in Canada and the United States, leading to . . .
- Tax cuts. Expect deep chops in federal taxes this year and in years to come as Ottawa seeks to raise Canada's productivity.
- Rising technology as the Internet becomes almost ubiquitous and more companies jump on the e-commerce way of doing things. That should lead to strong profit advances and robust markets.
- Demographics, which is the science of studying the population make-up. Today, Canada's dominant baby boom generation is moving into its peak income-generating and spending years. That's bullish for economic growth and also positive for financial markets as the boomers scramble to invest and make up for lost time.

The combination of all these factors is powerful, indeed. They should give you the confidence to see the next 10 or 15 years as an opportunity to invest in growth assets within your RRSP. After all, if you can get a 10% annual rate of return, the money inside your RRSP will double every seven years. If you get just a 4% return, it will take 18 long years to double what you have.

Source: The Globe and Mail

And never forget that the RRSP is one of the world's truly great investment vehicles. You can take assets you already own, put them inside an RRSP, and write half the value off your taxes. You can borrow to invest and get a refund equal to up to half the money you borrowed. You can contribute monthly to your retirement plan and actually take home more money since taxes on your paycheque are reduced. You can take that mortgage on your house and stick it inside your RRSP. You can use an RRSP to increase the amount of money you have available to buy a home. You can get 100% foreign content in your plan. You can split income with your spouse and have more money in your family. And lots, lots more.

So, come on with me into the new millennium. It's a wonderful time to be an investor, a perfect time to get on the right financial path, and the best time to get started.

"Martin backs off seniors plan"
—Globe and Mail headline, July 29, 1998

Chapter 1

Changes for 2000: After a bombshell, not all that much

Status quo reigns
Ottawa does the right thing
Previous damage

Whether you want to consider it the end of the decade, the twentieth century, or the second millennium, the past couple of years have been a wild ride, to say the least. Market volatility, the wayward Canadian dollar, the Asian mess, and the big but short-lived dump in October 1997, followed by another blown fuse in August 1998. And then we had Bill and Monica, the NATO police action in Yugoslavia, Y2K fear mongering, plus a host of other real and imagined impacts on the financial sector.

Despite all the calamities, the Dow and the TSE continue to reach for new heights. This past year the Dow soared past the 11,000 point mark and that for most of 1999, while the TSE performed much the same after breaking the 7000 mark.

Then there's our government. Earlier in the decade, it managed to tinker a fair bit with RRSP rules. However, for the past couple of years, at least since the 1996 budget, government interference has been minimal. And with the budget of 1999, no news is good news. There are a few things we would have liked the budget to include, like raising the

RRSP contribution limits or upping the foreign content limit, but let's count our blessings—it didn't give us a break, but it didn't take anything away either.

In fact, the only real thing to report on for this year is that there are a lot more foreign mutual funds available that are RRSP eligible. That means these can be added above and beyond the usual 20% foreign content limit. And with about 97% of the world's financial capitalization located outside Canada, it makes sense to expand your investment horizons.

For those who have forgotten or missed many of the changes and highlights of RRSP rule changes in past years, the following should bring you up to speed.

RECAP: BUDGETS PAST

When the federal government stopped borrowing money more than two years ago, we should have twigged that the deficit was well on its way to zero. And, sure enough, just a few months later, Paul Martin offered up his 1998 budget with the deficit gone and a surplus beginning to mount. Happy days.

Fresh with another firm majority in the election of 1997, it looked like the government—armed with its new fiscal accomplishments—might flex its muscles a little. But the 1998 budget, as it turned out, did very little all around, and focused instead on maintaining the economic status quo—taking the "if it ain't busted, why fix it?" stance.

Regardless, very little happened in the way of changes to RRSP rules. Let's face it, that was taken care of in the budgets just a year or two ago.

GOOD RIDDANCE

Probably one of the worst-conceived pieces of legislation, the proposed Seniors Benefit bit the dust just over a year ago. "Quite bluntly, in 1995 the option to fully preserve the OAS/GIS by simply choosing to fund it for the future did not practically exist. Today it does," said Finance Minister Martin in announcing the demise of his pet program.

But what many believe it came down to was that the government would never be able to sell the benign-sounding Seniors Benefit to the Canadian population at large. True, some low-income Canadians

You or your spouse will have to be enrolled in a qualifying education program—at least three months long—at an eligible institution. Disabled students can qualify for this program even if they pursue part-time studies. Again, the danger with this program, as with the Home Buyers' Plan, is that money taken out for a period of time means you're losing possibly years of tax-free compounding. If you can find educational financing somewhere else, do it.

Another aspect of the budget that can affect taxpayers was the introduction of a grant program—the Canada Education Savings Grant (CESG)—with which the government will boost Registered Education Savings Plan contributions. On the first $2000 contributed for each child under the age of 19, the government will add 20% directly to the RESP. An annual $2000 contribution will see the plan get a $400 boost from the feds. With the costs of future education predicted to soar, every little bit helps. Talk to your financial adviser about these plans. They have become more flexible over the years, and CESG will add to that allure. You do not get a tax refund for making a contribution, but the money inside the RESP can grow unfettered by taxes.

One of the more flexible features of some of these plans these days is the disposition of the funds if the child does not pursue higher education. In the old days, the money was lost into the scholarship pool. These days there are lots of options. The best option is that you can move some of the money into your RRSP. Prior to this budget you could roll over $40,000 into your retirement plan; now you can transfer up to $50,000. Any excess RESP money not able to fit into your RRSP will be subject to a 20% penalty (grant recovery) plus regular income tax.

Did you know . . .

. . . according to some estimates, children born today might need anywhere from $100,000 to $150,000 to finish four years of university?

NEW AND DIFFERENT IN 1998

As mentioned earlier, changes were few and far between. In fact there was just one major change: the restoration of lost RRSP room for individuals who leave a job and take with them a lump-sum payout from a

Source: Patrick Corrigan, Toronto Star

company pension plan. Of course, you wouldn't take that in a cheque (tax hit), but arrange to roll it over into your personal RRSP (see Chapter 12).

Usually, this lump sum is somewhat less than could have been contributed to a regular RRSP, and not be paying into a company pension plan and open to pension adjustment calculations.

OTHER MEMORABLE TWEAKING

The 1995 budget scaled back the maximum contribution level by $1000 to $13,500 until the end of 1997. But the 1997 budget drastically extended that freeze, which will mean that people earning over $75,000 a year will be paying more tax and contributing less to their plans.

The RRSP dollar limit is now fixed for the next five years (until 2004), although there was some talk after the last election of raising it before this century is out. Believe that when you see it. After the five-year freeze it is scheduled to rise to $14,500 in 2004 and then to $15,500 in 2005—a whole decade later than that level was supposed to have been achieved.

After that, contribution limits will be indexed to the average wage that has been barely moving higher through most of the nineties. The impact of this seemingly small change is actually quite enormous—especially for double-income, upper-middle-class families. Most of them will simply have less to retire on in the future, because while their ability to shelter savings is being cut, inflation is not.

DOLLAR LIMITS FOR CONTRIBUTIONS TO RRSPs

Year	Old rules	New rules
1996	$13,500	$13,500
1997	$13,500	$13,500
1998	$14,500	$13,500
1999	$15,500	$13,500
2000	Indexed	$13,500
2001		$13,500
2002		$13,500
2003		$13,500
2004		$14,500
2005		$15,500
2006		Indexed

No more carry-forward limit

This was good news of a sort. Since 1991, you have been allowed to carry forward RRSP contributions that you didn't, or couldn't, make for seven years.

This is a great idea, and a real blessing to people who have had a tough financial time over the last few years. The seven-year limit on carrying forward those missed contributions has been eliminated. At least for now.

Ottawa says this change recognizes the fact that many people go through long periods in their lives when they have no available cash for an RRSP—like early in their careers or while raising a family. The new rules allow them to catch up later in life, when they have a larger cash flow.

So, while this is an improvement, it also poses a danger. If people know they can catch up later, they may be inclined to spend their money now on a better lifestyle in the knowledge that no contribution room is being lost. And that would be a huge mistake

The real benefit comes not from how much you contribute to an RRSP, but when. Because RRSPs defer taxes until the plan is cashed in, it allows assets within the plan to compound free of tax—so the longer an asset is in there, the greater it grows.

Administration fees not tax-deductible

Now the annual administrative fee to run a self-directed plan is no longer deductible from your taxes when paid outside the plan. This fee is typically about $150 a year. As explained in the section on self-directed RRSPs, deductible fee or not, you must have one of these plans.

This is a typical nickel-and-dime move that will give the government a minimal amount in new revenues but that may make some people think twice about the benefit of having a self-directed RRSP.

In a post-budget interpretation, Revenue Canada says RRSP or RRIF administration fees paid outside the account will be considered a contribution to the RRSP, while fees paid inside will be considered a taxable withdrawal.

Counselling fees also not deductible

Here was a real sleeper—contained in a single paragraph buried in a technical Notice of Ways and Means Motion portion of the 1997 budget. And while it does not affect many people, those it does affect will be taking a significant tax whack.

Here's why: The money that wealthier people pay to have their RRSPs or RRIFs managed is no longer considered a deductible expense. For example, the average client of an investment counsellor will have a minimum RRSP of $500,000—which is not that much, considering the $1 million most of us middle-aged people will need to retire by the year 2015.

And with that much in an RRSP, it makes a lot of sense to have it professionally managed for maximum growth. But that doesn't come for free, and you can expect to pay a management fee of about 1% a year, about $5000 on $500,000.

For someone in the top tax bracket, this clarification now means an additional $2500 a year in tax owing—which effectively doubles the cost of having the RRSP managed.

This change will come to have a much greater significance in later years as baby boomers amass the capital they will need to retire with a half-decent income. Somebody today in their mid-thirties, making maximum RRSP contributions for the next 30 years will easily have a million-dollar investment to manage. And as more high-income earners today are downsized with large locked-in RRSPs that will grow over the years, they, too, will be hit with this tax that Ottawa tried so hard to hide in the back of the budget book.

No more retiring allowance

This was a stinker. A retirement allowance is money you get when you retire, quit, or are laid off. Up until the 1995 budget, you could roll over a big chunk of this cash directly into your RRSP. It is being phased out. A real crime. You can read the details in Chapter 12.

Two fewer years to contribute

Here is a big change. The length of time you can contribute money to an RRSP has been cut by two years.

At a certain point in your life, the rules say you have to stop putting money away for your old age, and start taking it out—and the best way of doing that is to convert the RRSP into a RRIF (more on that later). That age had been 71, and now it's 69.

This is very significant for many reasons. Obviously it will put more money into Ottawa's coffers as two years of tax deferral per person are swept away. This one change means we have all potentially lost $31,000 in tax-deductible savings.

It also looks like the first step in moving the whole concept of retirement age back, from 65 to 69. Don't be surprised if that ends up being the new age at which Canada Pension Plan benefits start to flow. And it won't stop there—the age at which you must stop contributing to an RRSP, and start taking money out, will eventually be reduced to 65 by the time the wave of baby boomers reaches that point.

This likely total drop of six years in the length of time you can make contributions means billions of dollars lost in potential tax savings for the 9 million people in my generation. It underscores the need today to take maximum advantage of the tax breaks that currently exist.

As a result of this change, it's essential for everyone to use the strategies I am presenting in this book, because the money you put into an RRSP will be working for you for a shorter period of time.

> ***Hardest hit are people who are now 55 or 60 years old. Not only will many of them not be getting the public pension supplement they were counting on, but the length of time they can prepare their own retirement savings has been eviscerated.***

The news is crystal clear: The great era of post-war social programs for everyone is gone. Of course, this comes at a time when being a senior citizen is harder than ever, thanks to the low inflation and plunging interest rates that have characterized the nineties. The average investment income for seniors has been dropping like a stone—down 10% in the latest year for which Statistics Canada has numbers.

I knew it would happen sooner or later.
Too many RRSP commercials!

Source: Bob Kain, Toronto Star

> **Did you know . . .**
> . . . that over the past 40 years the TSE 300 has had five years of double-digit drops? But, more importantly, it has had 22 years of double-digit gains.

Some of these recent changes are indeed daunting. But do not let any of this deter you—the changes simply underscore the need to take maximum advantage of the opportunities that remain. Your RRSP is still an awesome personal finance vehicle.

REMEMBER:

- Your RRSP is the best foundation of your entire investment program.
- The more the benefits are reduced, the more aggressive you must become.
- Maximize annual contributions and contribute early in the tax year—that can provide tens of thousands in extra assets.
- Can't find a lump sum to contribute? Then set up a monthly pre-authorized contribution and enjoy reduced taxes on your paycheque.
- Borrow the money. Most banks, trusts, credit unions, and many brokers or planners will lend you money at prime, or cheaper. Use the tax refund to pay down the loan.

"Every dollar that goes to service the debt is a dollar that cannot go to health care or tax relief."
—Paul Martin, Federal Minister of Finance

Chapter 2

Time marches on: Retirement crisis looms

Canada's economy today is in great shape. Corporate profits are up. Interest rates are idling nicely. The stock market continues to move ahead. Inflation has been squelched. Job markets continue to improve. Consumer confidence is in high gear. And the record number of corporate mergers that appear to be all the rage these days is not happening because these companies feel that the North American economy is going to shrink. In fact, when you look at the economic fundamentals in play, most of them add up to good times ahead.

Canada has been the leader in growth among the Western nations over the past couple of years, and it promises to repeat in some of the succeeding years. Life has been getting back to normal for most Canadians, a long-awaited release from the dismal recession blues that gripped so many during the first half of the nineties.

Happy times are here again. However (and there's always a however), while we're basking in the glow of these upbeat times—and we should bask, make no bones about it—we have to keep a watchful eye on the horizon.

These booming times should be a signal to most, if not all, Canadians that this is the golden opportunity we've been looking for to ensure security, stability, and serenity in the years to come. The sun is now shining—time to make hay and put something away for a rainy day. And that rainy day will inevitably come.

Over the next three decades, unbelievable changes are in store for Canadian society. Almost 10 million people will retire.

CANADA IS TURNING GREY

The number of seniors in Canada in the last 25 years has doubled. In the five-year period from 1991–96, the number of those over 65 increased 11.3% to well over 3.5 million. The fastest-growing age category over the next four years will be people 45 to 54 years old. In the same 1991–95 period, this age group enlarged itself by 15.5%. At the same time, the Canadian population grew only by 5.7%. But here's the most telling statistic: The fastest-growing age group over the next 20 years will be that of people over 80.

What does all this mean? Well, for one thing, the cost of health care will soar, by at least 50%. On top of that, most residential real estate will likely see its value erode. Governments will not be able to provide medical and pension benefits to the retired without drastically increasing taxes on working Canadians. Even increasing the Canada Pension Plan premiums by 70% and investing its revenues in the stock markets will not do the job. Not exactly the Utopia the Fathers of Confederation had in mind.

Tax increases of the size needed to support this situation are simply not possible.

Did you know . . .

. . . since 1990 Canadians have seen their disposable incomes drop by 9%? In the same period, Americans have seen their disposable incomes grow by 11%.

The Canadian Institute of Actuaries made the situation clear in a landmark 1994 report on the future, which was virtually ignored by the federal government: "We are asking a generation of Canadians to forego increases in their standard of living for the best part of their working lifetime. If real wages do not increase, we are asking them to accept a significant reduction in their standard of living."

Source: The Globe and Mail

In a chilling report a couple of years ago, the C.D. Howe Institute stated the obvious: Today's relatively well-off middle-aged and middle-class taxpayers will have to shoulder more burden. "Fiscal retrenchment should be focused so that more of the costs fall on well-to-do Canadians," concluded the report, *Beyond the Deficit: Generation X and Sustainable Debt.*

To do that, urged McMaster University economist William Scarth, government must, among other things:

- Toughen up pension rules for the wealthy
- Impose user fees
- End the universality of social programs

To a large extent, that is clearly the direction in which the federal government is heading. But taxing the wealthy alone is not enough. Scarth also argues that the future will be bleak even with Ottawa balancing its budget. He says that the feds have to run a surplus for the next decade, and vastly reduce the level of federal debt, if it hopes to deal with the coming retirement crunch.

This is why it is so critical that we all maximize RRSPs now—sheltering income from an increasing tax load, harnessing the power of rising financial markets, and building a defence against what could be a desperate time beyond the year 2015.

Proportionate to the size of its population, Canada has the biggest baby boom generation in the world. That means it will also likely have the biggest retirement crisis in the world.

Because of our relatively small population, Canada is overly dependent for its prosperity on trade. But our main trading partners also have aging populations, and face similar domestic problems.

A huge part of this problem is caring for the health of a rapidly aging population. Up to 90% of a person's total, lifetime medical costs can be incurred in the last six months of life.

> ***"The Baby Boom and subsequent baby bust have clearly created a tidal wave of shifting demographics. The transition from a young population to an old one will have profound consequences for our society . . ."***
>
> *—Canadian Institute of Actuaries*

Future costs of our current medical system are "unaffordable." Caring for today's population will cost today's taxpayers $1 trillion. "In the short run, until about the year 2000, the earning power of the Baby Boomers will go a long way towards supporting existing spending patterns," according to a report on health care by the Canadian Institute of Actuaries. "However, just after the turn of the century, the situation will change significantly. The leading edge of the age bulge reaches age 55 in the year 2000, and will begin to retire. That will have the two-edged effect that the productive base will begin to shrink and the high health care-user group will expand."

If nothing is done, each worker in 2031 will have to produce 60% more than he or she did in 1991 to care for senior dependants.

That, as you can well imagine, is totally impossible.

Did you know . . .

. . . that for a 45-year-old man to purchase long-term care insurance for his declining years, he would have to pay about $163 a month for 20 years? That would provide for up to $200 a day of long-term care at home or in a facility. But William M. Mercer Ltd. benefits consultant Malcolm Hamilton says that, while $200 may seem like a lot today, 30 years from now it may not even get you in the door of a long-term care institution.

Source: The Globe and Mail

So, the report called for an actual rationing of health care, along with a new emphasis on preventive medicine and a major cost control by government.

Will this happen? It's doubtful. Our baby boomer-dominated society and political structure is still funding health care on the pay-as-you-go basis—just like the endangered Canada Pension Plan. That means today's boomers are paying for the health care being consumed by their aged parents. Tomorrow Generation X will be faced with a stunning health bill to fund the hip replacements and prostate gland removals of legions of retired baby boomers.

Today, the estimated health care bill for people over 65 for the rest of their lives is $369 billion. But the health bill for all of the people who are working today, over the course of their lives, is $1 trillion—most of it payable in about 30 years.

But payable by whom? Well, we know the answer to that question. As Monique Jerome-Forget of the Institute for Research on Public Policy points out, "We all know by now that the current structure of Canada's fiscal policy is unsustainable from an economic standpoint. It is also immoral. We simply cannot continue borrowing against the future of our children."

Take a close look at the following graph showing the age structure of the country. Today it looks close to what the "proper" age structure of any society should be—a pyramid, with more younger people at the bottom, tapering to narrow bands of older citizens at the top.

ACTUAL AGE STRUCTURE – CANADA

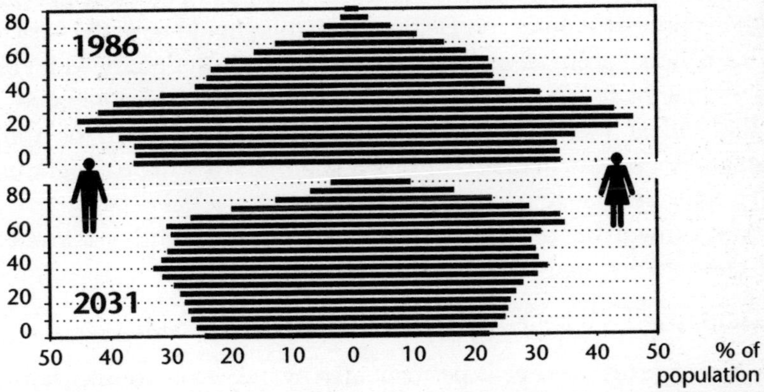

Unbelievable change is taking place in the makeup of Canada's population. In less than 35 years the largest segment of the population will be 65-year-old women. The next largest group will be 70-year-old women.

Source: Canadian Institute of Actuaries

But this pyramid is about to disappear, turning into a mushroom—incredibly, with thicker bands of old people in their sixties and seventies at the top, dwarfing the younger population below.

By 2031—32 years from now, when today's youngest baby boomers contemplate retirement—the largest single population group will be women aged 65. The second-largest group will be women aged 70. There will be, in fact, more 75-year-old women around than girls under 10 years of age.

> ***With life expectancies far greater than most men, women have to be even more concerned and proactive in their attempts to provide for their later years. Yet many, if not most, are not taking any action now to ensure they are not marginalized as they join the ranks of the elderly.***

A study by the Harris Bank, Chicago, found that of the women surveyed (all over age 30 and with incomes in excess of US$40,000), most were still not saving enough for retirement, even though they make almost double the average per capita income. It's no different up here north of the 49th. Most Canadian women are not, nor are encouraged to be, aggressive enough to secure their financial future.

In fact, most Canadians, men and women, are not tackling the issue with the priority it deserves. Dealing with this should be at the very top of the national political agenda. The fact that it is not pretty well guarantees that the future is going to be a dark place for the unprepared.

Retirement financing for today's baby boomers will be tough enough. For people in their twenties and thirties, it will be a nightmare unless drastic change occurs.

According to the Institute for Research on Public Policy, correcting the intergenerational imbalance would mean:

- Gutting today's benefits for seniors—ripe for a revolt.
- Raising taxes each year permanently by 1.2%—revolting, but not out of the question.
- Cutting government purchases by 10.4%—a revolutionary idea, but what are the odds of it happening?

Without that kind of action, this is how the tax and benefit scorecard looks:

Age and sex now	Get more in benefits	Pay more in taxes
Newborn boy		$131,200
Newborn girl		$56,700
25-year-old man		$290,000
25-year-old woman		$136,000
65-year-old man	$121,400	
65-year-old woman	$108,100	

Canada's population profile makes this about the worst country in the world to have the kind of social programs that we do, namely, pay-as-you-go. The tidal wave of aging baby boomers will drive that home in a dramatic, destructive way.

A person born in 1911, for example, will get a 22.4% return on the money paid out in Canada Pension Plan contributions. A person born today will get a rate of return of about 1.5% on all the money he or she will pay into the Canada Pension Plan during a whole lifetime. As the

WHAT YOU PAY, WHAT YOU GET

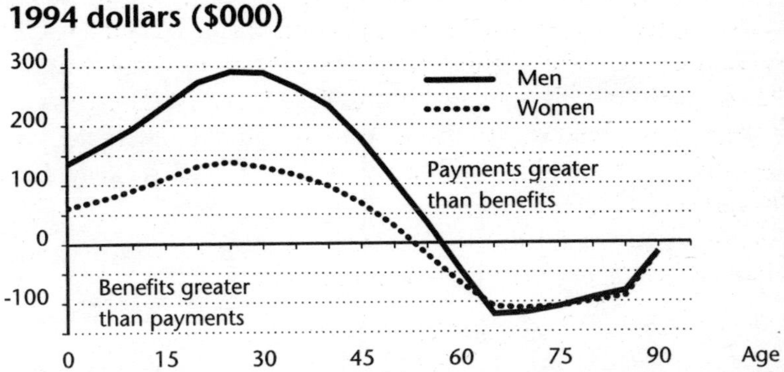

Today's 20-year-old will pay hundreds of thousands of dollars more in taxes than he or she will ever collect in benefits, while today's 65-year-old will receive $121,000 more than he or she contributes. Generation X has good reason to be angry.

Source: Institute for Research on Public Policy

Canadian Institute of Actuaries pointed out in its report on the future of the public pension plan, it was "enacted in 1965, when Canada was nearing the end of an unprecedented 20-year economic boom. The economy had grown quickly in real terms. Interest rates, nominal and real, were low.

"Economists believed that this environment, and the concurrent baby boom, would endure and that pay-as-you-go systems could ride a wave of prosperity."

Ironically, the great baby boom ended about 18 months after the Canada Pension Plan was created—with its whole funding premise being that the babies would never stop coming.

As a matter of fact . . .

. . . asking Canadians for an extra 70% in CPP premiums may not do the trick, says Lloyd Atkinson of Perigree Investment Counsel Inc. He warns that the retirement age might have to go up to 67, that benefits may have to be clawed back even more than expected, and that further down the road the age of retirement could again be raised higher.

"IF A SHARE PRICE FALLS IN THE FOREST AND THERE ISN'T AN ANALYST THERE TO EXPLAIN IT, DID IT EVER REALLY HAPPEN?"

Source: Brown, Toronto Star

With these dire warnings, and given the population make-up, the CPP is cooked. Any serious retirement planning you do should not include public pension income.

Yes, financial markets will rise and the North American economy will improve for at least a decade, maybe longer. But beyond that, things will get a lot murkier and tougher. Especially for the majority of people my age who are not prepared for what we know is coming.

> ***We are powerless to reverse the aging of the Canadian population. So we must do more to prepare for it, and then to continue building our financial assets while in retirement.***

Based on current evidence, taxes will likely go up in the future, not down. The level of government support will fall. Most of today's middle-aged, middle-class people will receive no public pensions.

There will be a health care crisis so long as the country tries to keep a universal, public, free-access system. Faced with millions more elderly people, care will either have to be or the system will have to be at least partially privatized. Either way, it's going to cost a lot more to get sick in 2020 than it does today.

NOT ALL NEWS IS BAD

RRSP investors today face wonderful, almost unparalleled, opportunities to make their money grow. The aging population means lower inflation, and that will also knock down interest rates over the long term.

The value of real assets—real estate, gold, Porsches—will decline, and the value of financial assets will rise. Quality stocks, bonds, and mutual funds will catapult higher in value as money flows out of real assets.

At the same time, the baby boom generation is entering its peak earning and spending years. A growing number of people in this age group have the mortgage paid off, giving them more disposable income. And as millions of people hit age 50 at the same time, starting in the year 2000, they will do to stocks, bonds, and funds what they did to real estate in the eighties—driving valuations higher as they scramble to invest in the same places.

If you know that now, at the beginning of the new millennium, then I think you know where to invest.

And you know where not to invest.

This is a time for the middle-aged and older to be systematically removing equity from residential real estate and transferring it to financial assets. For many people, this is a shocking notion. It means borrowing against your paid-up house and getting the money into assets like equities and mutual funds. This does not mean selling your home—although for many that is a good option—but rather diversifying through a home equity loan. Canadians have 70% of their net worth in residential real estate, which is far too much. Besides, most residential real estate faces a bleak long-term future.

Your house has probably gone down in value, especially if you bought it in the mid- to late eighties. It's going to take a long time yet before you see those values again, if ever. Meanwhile, equity-based mutual funds that track stock market performance have been growing by double digits. These booming financial markets will continue to make tracks upward. For people serious about growing their wealth, the timing could hardly be better.

And there is no easier way to accomplish this magic than within an RRSP. Here's how . . .

"Many people don't appreciate how important RRSPs are until the later stages of their careers. There's generally a great shift in awareness and sense of urgency as people hit their late 40s. Then they start to scramble to maximize their RRSPs."

—Peter Volpé, Senior Vice President, Integra Capital Management

Chapter 3

Just the FAQs (Frequently Asked Questions)

- **A definition**
- **Eligibility**
- **Contribution limits**
- **Deadlines**
- **Tax savings**
- **What can go in**
- **Multiple RRSPs**
- **RRSP loans**
- **Foreign content**
- **Buying a house**
- **Income splitting**
- **Transfers**
- **Death, taxes, and divorce**

About two-thirds of Canadians don't have an RRSP. In fact, many people still have no idea what an RRSP is. Nor do they realize how it can improve their financial circumstances today, and provide retirement years free from financial worry.

Like many others, I should be surprised by this fact. But I'm not. After all, this isn't stuff that is taught in schools, and most of the companies handling RRSPs do precious little to inform and educate the masses in a concise, straightforward manner.

The complexities and ramifications of an RRSP can boggle the mind, but that's why you have a financial adviser. Still, Canadians need to know that an RRSP is basically a very simple item.

IN THE BUBBLE

Imagine, if you will, a large bubble where you can stack your financial assets. The assets are then free to grow and compound within this bubble that shields them from taxes.

That bubble is called an RRSP, and it is not a product that you buy at the bank. But thousands—maybe millions—of Canadians believe just that. So, they happily dump billions of dollars into low-yield savings instruments like GICs, never even knowing there is a world of sexy alternatives.

An RRSP is not a thing; it's a process—a convenient and flexible way to shelter investments from tax. It was created in 1957—even before we had a public pension plan—and it was always intended to be the principal pillar of retirement planning. But it's only been in the past decade or so that people have come to realize just how valuable, versatile, and powerful an RRSP can be.

As a matter of fact . . .
. . . 50% of Canadians claim to have a financial adviser, yet only one-third of these individuals actually have a financial plan for retirement. So says a survey conducted by A.C. Nielsen on behalf of the Canadian Imperial Bank of Commerce. The poll also discovered that 80% of those aged 18 to 35 have no plan at all.

Still, only 5 million of us have started saving using this wonderful tool. The rest are paying more taxes than they have to. Their investments are underperforming—victims of inflation, or lack of it. And most of these people are in deep denial.

Here is all you really need to know:

WHAT IS AN RRSP?

A fair question, which most Canadians can't answer. A Registered Retirement Savings Plan or RRSP lets you defer taxes on money you save today. The idea is to encourage you to save by letting you put off paying those taxes until you retire—when most are in a lower tax bracket and will pay less tax on those savings.

The benefits of opening an RRSP and contributing to it every month or year are enormous:

- First, all of the money put in the plan is deducted from your taxable income, meaning most people get big tax refund cheques.
- Second, taxable investments can be put in your RRSP, and will grow in value tax-free. I don't care what anybody tells you about investments, there is no faster way to build wealth than doing it within an RRSP.
- Third, on retirement, you can roll your RRSP assets over into a RRIF (Registered Retirement Income Fund), which further defers taxes, as long as you take a minimal amount out of the plan every year.
- Fourth, you can save a bundle on lifetime taxes. By deferring taxation until later in life—and using an RRSP to split income with your less-taxed spouse—you will, in most cases, be taxed at a lower marginal rate.

Simply put: This is the best leg-up on the future you're going to get. In fact, the RRSP rules are so generous, flexible, and accommodating it's hard to believe they exist in this country, where we are taxed to death, and quite often after that event.

WHO QUALIFIES FOR AN RRSP?

Anybody who earns income can contribute to an RRSP until the end of the year in which they turn 69. If you turn 70 in 2001, then you have until December 31, 2000, to contribute to your plan. Then you should convert it into a RRIF and start taking money out. You can also continue putting money into your spouse's RRSP, no matter what your age, until that spouse turns 69. There is no minimum age—so long as you earn income. You should, however, file a tax return, even in years when no taxes are due.

HOW MUCH CAN YOU CONTRIBUTE?

That depends on how much income you make. If you work for a company that has a pension plan, your maximum contribution for the 1999 tax year is 18% of your 1998 income, minus a pension adjustment—to a maximum of $13,500.

For those without a company plan, the limit is 18% of income to a maximum of $13,500. To reach that contribution level, your income has to be $75,000, putting you in the top 6% of Canadian earners.

WHAT IF I MISS A YEAR?

Relax—you can catch up later on missed contributions, but you can never catch up on the tax-free income those contributions could have earned during all the time you did not join in.

The 1997 budget removed a restriction limiting the ability to carry forward missed contributions for only seven years—now it is unlimited. But don't use that as an excuse not to chip in. The ability to catch up on missed contributions might not be around forever (see Chapter 13).

WHAT IF I CONTRIBUTE TOO MUCH?

You can overcontribute without penalty, so long as it doesn't exceed $2000 during your lifetime. A few years back, that limit was $8000, but it was drastically scaled back in the 1995 budget. It might disappear completely in the future—so take advantage now.

There's no tax deduction for an overcontribution, but it can still grow tax-free within your plan. And you can use it in future years for future RRSP payments.

Overcontributions can be withdrawn, but in most cases you will be charged withholding tax, which you claim back on your income tax return by filing Form 3012A.

If your overcontribution exceeds the $2000 limit, Revenue Canada will box your ears, charging you a penalty of 1% a month on the extra money until it is removed. Children under 18 at the beginning of the year can't make an overcontribution. They can do so the year following the year in which they turn 19.

WHEN CAN YOU MAKE A CONTRIBUTION?

Any time is good. Earlier is better. And doing it monthly is great.

Many people think they can only make a contribution in January or February 2000—the "RRSP season" for the 1999 tax year. But aggressive investors can start loading up their 1999 contributions beginning in January 1999.

RRSP season has evolved because people leave doing important things until the last minute, and the deadline for making a contribution that will earn you a tax break is within 60 days of the end of the year. That means the deadline for saving on 1999 taxes is February 29, 2000.

Of course, you mustn't miss that deadline. But you should make every effort to contribute as early in the year as possible for that particular tax year, not the previous one. This means your money compounds for an extra year. Just by changing the day on which you make your contribution you can be tens of thousands of dollars ahead in retirement.

Now, if it's hard to find a big pile of extra money each year, contribute monthly—and at the same time see your paycheque taxes reduced. A regular RRSP payment soon becomes like a car loan—something you forget about.

Did you know . . .

. . . if you are 32 years old and put $4300 into your RRSP every year until 65—and it earns an average of 8%—you'll have more than $600,000 on retirement? If you start doing this at age 20, by 65 you can have more than twice that amount—about $1.5 million.

WHAT'S THE TAX BREAK?

It's a big one. And, unlike most of the rest of things in life, the more money you make, the bigger the tax break is.

The entire contribution amount is deducted from your taxable income. If you contribute $5000 and you are in the 40% tax bracket, you save $2000; if you are in the 54% tax bracket, you save $2700.

Of course, this could change in the future. The tax credit system could be applied, which would reduce the tax break for upper-income earners (see Chapter 13).

WHAT CAN GO IN MY RRSP BUBBLE?

A huge number of financial assets can go into an RRSP, but most people—wrongly—put their retirement savings into GICs or savings bonds. These offer no risk, but these days they offer only very low rates of return. Investors who don't want any risk could get a far higher rate of return with government strip bonds (see Chapter 10). Other things you can put in your RRSP include:

- Mutual funds
- Term deposits
- Canadian stocks
- Corporate strip bonds
- Federal and provincial government bonds
- Crown corporation bonds
- Foreign government bonds
- Limited partnership units
- Labour-sponsored venture capital funds
- Small business shares
- Mortgages
- Your own mortgage

"Please stay on the line, sir, and someone will soon be available to confuse you . . ."

Source: David Brown, Toronto Star

WHAT CAN'T BE IN MY RRSP?

Real estate, precious metals, foreign currency, art, antiques, put options, commodities, or futures. That pretty well covers it. But existing rules allow you to put real estate or gold mutual funds or stocks in your RRSP. You can have bonds or other securities denominated in foreign currencies in there as well.

HOW MANY PLANS CAN I HAVE?

Just as many as you want. You can have several RRSPs at several financial institutions—but I wouldn't recommend it. Each plan—if it's self-directed (and it should be) costs about $150 a year to administer, and that money is no longer tax-deductible. In addition, there are often transaction fees. And human nature being what it is, it's sometimes hard to manage multiple plans.

My advice? Just have one, big, self-directed plan—managed by a smart financial adviser—and invest in equity mutual funds, stocks, federal and provincial government bonds, Crown corporation bonds, and corporate bonds. With one plan, costs are kept in check, and it's easy to measure the plan's monthly performance.

CAN I BORROW FOR MY RRSP?

Yes, but the interest is not tax deductible. That used to be the case, but loans taken out now to make an RRSP contribution are not tax deductible.

But that doesn't mean you should not borrow. Indeed, borrow all you need to make the annual maximum allowable contribution. Here's why:

- Most financial institutions will give you an RRSP loan at their best rate—usually prime. Many brokerages or financial planning firms will even get you money below the prime rate, as long as they are managing your portfolio.
- An RRSP contribution, usually, will net you a fat tax refund. Just take that refund cheque to where you borrowed the money and use it to pay down a major part of that loan.
- Any kind of astute investing—say, in conservatively managed, equity-based mutual funds—will earn tax-free returns well in excess of the cost of borrowing.
- As a general rule of thumb, if you can pay off the RRSP loan within a year—by the time you need to take out another one—you're doing just fine.

Here is an example of why it's smart to borrow so you can make your maximum annual RRSP contribution. Let's say you have $5000 to invest, but under the rules you could put in $10,000. How much further ahead would you be by borrowing the other $5000?

	Invest $5,000	Invest $10,000 (with a loan)
Tax refund at 40% rate	$2,000	$4,000
Invest in a government bond yielding 7%	350	700
You're ahead by this much	$2,350	$ 4,700
Use refund to pay down loan		−4,000
Repay rest of loan at 7%		−1,070
Net gain	$2,000	−1,070
RRSP assets	$5,350	$10,700
Total assets	$7,350	$ 9,630

Did you know . . .

. . . that London Life Insurance estimates that a couple can currently have a comfortable retirement on an annual after-tax income of $20,350? For an above-average retirement, a couple will need $37,000 a year in after-tax income, while $81,400 can deliver a luxurious lifestyle.

IS FOREIGN CONTENT NECESSARY?

Smart people know not to have all their eggs in one basket—or all their wealth in Canadian dollars. For instance, even though the sovereignty issue in Quebec has been turned down to simmer, there could still be a referendum down the line.

That means short-term interest rates will jump and the dollar will tumble—just like every other time there's been a national unity crisis.

So it's a no-brainer to put some of your dollars into foreign investments. The rules allow you to have up to 20% of the total book value of your RRSP in foreign securities. There are also many more funds now coming into the market that offer foreign content but that are 100% RRSP eligible. Check them out with your adviser. There's more on foreign content in Chapter 5.

CAN MY RRSP HELP BUY A HOUSE?

It sure can, under the Home Buyers' Plan. As a first-time buyer you can withdraw up to $20,000 for a down payment or, together with your spouse, up to $40,000. The money has to be paid back into the plan, but you get 15 years to do that.

Simply put, this is the only way I know of getting $40,000 free of tax and without interest.

However, the most important thing to remember is that money removed from your RRSP is no longer compounding tax-free. For more on real estate strategies see Chapters 7 and 8.

CAN I SPLIT INCOME WITH AN RRSP?

Absolutely. And you should. You do not want to end up in retirement with the bulk of your family assets in the name of the person who pays the most tax—but that is exactly what happens to most Canadians.

Typically, the husband makes the most money, makes the most investments, and ends up in the top marginal tax bracket, because the couple's income is flowing in through his fingers. That family could vastly improve its income level and standard of living by simply shifting assets into the name of the lower-taxed spouse.

You're allowed to contribute to your husband or wife's RRSP, up to the same level you could put money into your own plan. After a short period of time, those assets then belong to the other person and, when cashed in, are taxed at his or her rate, not yours.

CAN I TRANSFER BETWEEN DIFFERENT PLANS?

Yes, Revenue Canada imposes no penalties for transfers, but switches can often be a real hassle because financial institutions get cranky about sending money to other institutions. Expect to pay a fee to the bank or trust when you move RRSP money, and expect delays. Make sure the bank has the paperwork long before the switch is to take place. Then hope for the best.

TIP: The company you are transferring your RRSP to will be happy for the business—probably happy enough to pay the fee charged by the transferring company. Be sure to ask about this before committing.

WHAT HAPPENS IF I DON'T LIVE FOREVER?

Hey, this is Canada—when you die, you pay tax. Upon death an RRSP is deemed to be cashed out, which means your estate pays big bucks in tax because the whole amount is added to your taxable income in that year.

This is why you should not write "Estate" on that part of the RRSP application that asks you who should be the beneficiary. You can roll over your entire RRSP assets, free of tax, to your spouse simply by naming him or her as the beneficiary.

Or you can give any infirm children or grandchildren under 18 who are dependent on you the same tax-free gift, without having to pay probate fees. Or you can designate your RRSP to buy an annuity to look after a healthy dependent child or grandchild until he or she becomes 18.

Now, what happens if you do not have a spouse or offspring, and designate somebody else as beneficiary? There is no way to transfer those assets to somebody without tax implications. So your bank or trust company will treat that as a simple withdrawal of the RRSP and send your estate a T4RSP tax slip. Then your estate has to pay what is probably going to be a very large tax bill.

This becomes tricky.

If you have $100,000 in an RRSP and another $100,000 in assets when you die, and you want to leave the money equally to two friends or relatives, you have to do it carefully. If you name one as the beneficiary of your RRSP, then a tax bill of about $50,000 will be payable—not by the beneficiary, but by the estate.

That means the beneficiary will get the full $100,000, but the second person, named as the inheritor of your estate, will only get $50,000, after the tax bill is paid.

So, in this case, it would be fairer to name the estate as the beneficiary of the RRSP, and the two friends or relatives as the joint inheritors. That way, at least, the tax owing would be shared equally by both (but probate would be liable).

Other things to consider:

- If you die without designating your spouse as the beneficiary of your RRSP, but if he or she is the beneficiary of your estate (as spelled out in your will), then it's still okay. Your spouse can get the money by filling out Form T2019 and the RRSP assets will be transferred, tax-free.

- Children stop being children, as Revenue Canada sees it, when they turn 18. That means beyond that age you cannot roll your RRSP assets over to them without being taxed (the exception is for an infirm child or grandchild, regardless of age). That means you should review your will and RRSP documents on a regular basis.
- Ditto with the marriage. The divorce rate is astonishingly high in this country and, by law, retirement assets are divided equally upon divorce, because, like the house, cottage, car, and furniture, they are considered "family assets" under most provincial laws. Marriage breakdown is unique in that it is the only situation in which both RRSPs and pension assets are divided equally between husband and wife.

That can lead to a situation in which, to keep his own company pension, a man may have to sign over RRSP assets in his name to his spouse. Or the funds in an RRSP in a wife's name could be swapped for the family real estate, if they were of nearly equal value. Sound messy? It sure can be.

And if a marriage collapse is on the horizon, the spouse who's been making contributions might want to stop—saving his or her contribution "room" for future years when the separation is history and the RRSP sharing is over.

But all of this doesn't mean your former spouse has to get the other half if you die first. Make sure you change the beneficiary designation at the bank or trust or brokerage where your RRSP lives. Divorce will automatically change the designation in your will, but not at the institution. And if you remarry, ensure that your new spouse is the new beneficiary.

That will help get things off on the right foot.

As a matter of fact . . .

. . . a Scotiabank poll found that fewer than 40% of Canadians with RRSPs planned to maximize their contributions in 1998. Yet, the survey found that 85.6% who were not retired expected their standard of living to be the same or better in retirement. Maybe they're using new math.

JUST TO RECAP:

- An RRSP is not a product; it is a process.
- An RRSP defers tax on your investments, allowing you to pay that tax in retirement when you should be in a lower tax bracket.
- Monthly RRSP contributions can lower taxes on your paycheque.
- A yearly RRSP contribution will see you get a tax refund.
- You can contribute to an RRSP until the end of the year in which you turn 69.
- There is no minimum age—so long as you earn income.
- You should file a tax return, even in years when no taxes are due.
- The contribution limit is 18% of the previous year's income to a maximum of $13,500.
- Payments into a company pension plan are deducted from this contribution room.
- Missed contributions can be made at any time in future years.
- You can make a total lifetime overcontribution of $2000.
- There is no tax refund on an overcontribution.
- You can contribute to your RRSP at any time.
- For any particular tax year, your contribution must be made by the end of February of the subsequent year.
- The amount of your refund depends on your particular tax bracket.
- A whole range of investment products are RRSP eligible.
- Certain investments are not RRSP eligible.
- You can have more than one RRSP, but it's best to just have one self-directed plan.
- Interest on a loan taken out for RRSP investing is not tax deductible.
- Most financial institutions will offer RRSP loans at their best rate—prime.

- Your RRSP is allowed to contain up to 20% in foreign securities.
- First-time home buyers can withdraw up to $20,000 ($40,000 with spouse) to buy a house.
- You can contribute to your spouse's RRSP, earning a tax refund while splitting income.
- Transferring plans from one financial institution to another is okay with Revenue Canada.
- Do not write "Estate" as the beneficiary of your RRSP—doing so results in a big tax hit—name your spouse.

"Too many Canadians are not saving enough for their retirement, hoping that government-supported plans will carry them through. The sad truth is that even if government plans are around by the time we want to retire, they will probably pay us about $13,700 a year—far below what most of us expect to live on."

—Maureen Loweth, Vice President and National Director, The Fidelity Institute

Chapter 4

Contribute early and often to cut tax and build wealth

Pension plan considerations
Calculate your earned income
Reduce tax—build wealth

You are allowed to contribute a certain percentage of your earned income every year into an RRSP, to the allowable maximum. Earned income, by the way, is money you earned by working or having rental income, not money your investments have brought in. Only a tiny number of Canadians actually contribute their RRSP maximum each year, because they either don't earn enough or, if they do, don't have that much extra cash.

One of the very best RRSP strategies possible is to contribute to your plan early in the tax year. That means you should make your 2000 contribution on Tuesday, January 4, 2000.

How much are you are allowed in that year? Your annual T4 slip from your employer arrives in February. You may not really know for sure how much money you will make in 2000. And Revenue Canada

Source: The Toronto Star

will not be sending you a statement of how much you can put into the RRSP, based on 1999 income, until some time in the summer, by way of a Notice of Assessment.

The simple way is to guess—after all, you can fine-tune your plan later in the year when Revenue Canada does notify you.

Or, you can call Revenue Canada's TIPS line. It is listed in the blue pages (grey pages in Manitoba) of your phone book under Revenue Canada, Taxation (Can 48 section). Have last year's tax return handy, along with your social insurance number. The computer will talk to you for a while and then tell you your limit, including missed past contributions.

But if you are one of those hands-on people who want the accurate and complicated approach, well, here we go.

IF YOU DON'T HAVE A COMPANY PENSION PLAN

In 2000, you can contribute 18% of the money you earned in 1999, to a maximum of $13,500. Plus, you can catch up on past contributions, as well as overcontribute once to the limit of $2000.

IF YOU DO HAVE A COMPANY PENSION PLAN

It's the same procedure, but you need to take into account your pension adjustment, which can be found in Box 52 of the T4 slip you get in February. You can contribute 18% of your earned income to a maximum of $13,500, less the pension adjustment amount.

HOW TO DETERMINE YOUR "EARNED INCOME"

This is the tricky part, because some of your income is allowed when calculating RRSP contribution limits, and some is not.

Here is what qualifies as "earned income":

- Employment earnings
- Self-employment earnings
- Rental income (after expenses, like mortgage payments)
- Royalties and advances (authors and inventors)
- Research grants
- CPP and QPP disability payments
- Taxable long-term disability payments
- Employee profit-sharing plan allocations
- Supplementary employment-insurance benefits
- Alimony and child support
- Director's fees
- Any taxable benefits showing up on your T4 slip

And here is a partial list of income that does not qualify you to increase your RRSP contribution limit:

- Employment-insurance benefits
- CPP or QPP retirement benefits
- Investment interest (GICs, etc.)
- Capital gains
- Dividend income
- Pension income
- Business income as limited partner
- Scholarships or bursaries

Now, once you have added together all your earned income, reduce that amount by subtracting a few things, including:

- Union dues
- Alimony payments
- Self-employment losses
- Professional dues
- Deductible employment expenses
- Rental losses

And there you have it: your "earned income." Multiply it by 18%, then deduct your pension adjustment from that amount (if applicable) and that is your allowed 1999 RRSP contribution, so long as it does not exceed $13,500. Add to it any unused contribution "room" from the past, and subtract any overcontributions beyond the $2000 limit. Here's a ready-made worksheet to help you get to that bottom line:

CONTRIBUTION CALCULATOR

To determine your 2000 RRSP contribution limit

1. ***Determine your 1999 "earned income" using the worksheet included here.***

2. ***Multiply that earned income by 18%. That amount, or $13,500—whichever is less—is your contribution base.***

3. ***Find out your pension adjustment amount—listed on the T4 slip your employer will send you by the end of February 2000. If you want to make an earlier contribution, your payroll department can estimate the amount.***

4. ***Subtract the pension adjustment from your RRSP contribution base. That's how much you can put into your plan in 2000.***

If you are not a member of a company pension plan, then it is simpler. Just take 18% of your total earned income in 1999 and contribute that amount, or $13,500, whichever is less.

And if you earned more than $75,000 in 1999, you don't need to do the 18% calculation. Just use $13,500 as your limit if you do not have a company pension, or $13,500 less the pension adjustment if you do.

WORKSHEET FOR CALCULATING EARNED INCOME

Add together:	Line on 1999 tax return	Amount
Total employment earnings (T4 slips)	101-104	______
Net rental income	104	______
Alimony or child care income	128	______
Self-employment income	135-143	______
Taxable disability payments	114,152	______
Employee profit-sharing allocation	104	______
Research grants	104	______
Supplementary employment-insurance benefits	104	______
Author or inventor royalties	104	______
Taxable benefits (from T4)		______
Total		

Subtract from that:

Union or professional dues	212	________
Alimony or support payments	220	________
Rental losses	126	________
Self-employment losses	135-143	________
Tax-deductible expenses	229	________
Total		________
1999 earned income		________

WEALTH BUILDER NO. 1: SAVE TAXES

For the second year in a row the federal government has run a surplus. But just as they did the year before, the feds brought down a truly unspectacular budget in 1999. The level of personal taxation is still expected to rise by $360 million in 1999–2000, much of it through increased Canada Pension Plan contributions.

The deficit has been routed, but the country's debt (the total of our deficits) will rise to $649 billion from $578 billion last year. And it will cost a stunning $49 billion this year just to pay the interest on that debt.

Source: The Globe and Mail

> **As a matter of fact . . .**
> . . . a billion is a thousand million. It looks like this: $1,000,000,000. If you spent $1200 a day since Christ was born, you would not have spent a billion dollars yet. That wouldn't happen, actually, until July 2283.

Almost $50 billion a year in interest must be borne by about 10 million taxpayers, who contribute more into the system than they take out. The Canadian middle class represents beasts of financial burden—the easiest of targets for the folks who write federal budgets.

This is precisely why Canadian taxes are not going down any time soon, and it is why tax planning is one of the most important things you can possibly do to help ensure your financial future. And nothing reduces taxes like an RRSP contribution.

Face it: The cost of living in this Utopia is intense. If you make more than $60,000 a year, you are considered rich. That's when the top marginal tax rate clicks in and suddenly you are giving over 53 cents of every dollar you earn. Compared to other countries, especially the United States, with whom our tax system competes, we are seriously out of step.

In the United States, the top marginal tax rate is 39.6%, not 53%. And you don't pay that rate at an income level of just $60,000—instead you start paying top bucks when you are earning more than $256,500 a year (if single or, if married, when filing a joint return). So, it's clear: Tax planning is four or five times more important to Canadians than it is to Americans.

Our high taxes have resulted in a burgeoning underground economy. It has also spawned a new generation of tax cheats infatuated with the idea of sending their wealth offshore. Revenue Canada's efforts to counter that will cost middle-class taxpayers at least $70 million more this year.

The truth is, you don't need to be a tax cheat or evader to drastically reduce the amount of tax you pay. There are many ways to legally increase your income by decreasing your level of taxation.

Too many people pay more tax than the law requires. I was shocked when I became Minister of National Revenue to see how many taxpayers overpaid. They missed obvious deductions and exemptions. They didn't use legal tax shelters like RRSPs. They didn't split their income with their spouses and children. They didn't make their mortgages tax deductible. They didn't use any of these powerful RRSP strategies that can save thousands of dollars with just a couple of phone calls.

A lot of wealthy Canadians know about these strategies, and use them. In fact, in 1996 a record amount of money went into RRSPs—well over $26 billion—and 1997 and 1998 figures are comparable. But the relative number of people contributing did not go up—it's just the same third of Canadians who have it figured out.

Too many others are walking away from their tax bills, changing their names, declaring bankruptcy, or working for cash. The Canadian middle class seems to be breaking in two—those who are cashing in RRSPs and those who are pumping them full.

As thousands more walk away from their tax obligations, it leaves a dwindling number of middle-class Canadians to pay the freight. Now just 30% of Canadian families pay more than 62% of all taxes.

So, the simplest survival rule for 2000 and beyond is this: It's far easier to save money than to make money.

And this is what the RRSP—North America's best tax shelter—is all about.

The amount of money you will save on your 1999 taxes by making an RRSP contribution by February 29, 2000, depends on how much money you put in, and on your marginal tax rate.

The marginal tax rate is determined by the combination of federal and provincial income taxes where you live, and varies slightly from province to province. Here is how Canadians are taxed federally.

CANADIAN TAX RATES

Income level	Tax rate	Including surtax
$29,590 or less	17%	17.5%
$29,591 to $59,180	26%	26.8%
$59,181 to $62,195	29%	29.9%
Above $62,196	29%	31.3%

Added to this are provincial income taxes, which are levied as a percentage of federal tax payable. The rates range from a low of 45% in the Northwest Territories to a high of 69% in Newfoundland. In addition, most provinces have high-income surtaxes, and three (Alberta, Manitoba, and Saskatchewan) also impose flat taxes. As a result, the maximum combined tax rates range from 44.3% in the Northwest Territories to a high of 54.1% in British Columbia.

To calculate your tax reduction, simply multiply the amount you can contribute to your RRSP by your marginal tax rate.

For example, if you live in Nova Scotia, and had taxable income in 1999 of $68,000, and can make the maximum RRSP contribution of $12,240, this is how to determine your refund:

$$\$12{,}240 \times 48.5\% = \$5{,}936$$

The current system clearly favours people with higher incomes, because the RRSP contribution reduces taxable income, and therefore the tax payable. The more money you earn, the higher your tax bracket. And the higher the tax bracket you are in, the more you save by making a contribution.

There is a strong possibility this may change in the future, with Ottawa going to a system of tax credits, which would address the idea some have that wealthier Canadians are getting a disproportionate RRSP break. But the system as it is today recognizes the fact that upper-income Canadians shoulder a massive amount of the tax burden.

The most significant thing upper-middle-class taxpayers can do to increase their family incomes—freeing up tens of thousands of dollars to invest in today's booming financial markets—is to maximize annual RRSP contributions.

The sooner money is put into your plan, the faster it will compound. And recognize that basic investing should start inside the RRSP bubble. If you have $10,000 to invest in mutual funds, first put it inside a self-directed RRSP. That will earn you a tax refund of $4000 to $5000. Now you have thousands more to put into funds, both inside and outside the retirement savings plan. Next year you can use a portion of your contribution room to move funds into your RRSP from outside it. And just for doing that, you will receive another tax rebate cheque of about $2000.

Meanwhile your funds should give you double-digit annual returns. So, one year after investing $10,000 in a self-directed RRSP, you will have maybe $17,000 in assets.

How much would your salary have to be increased to take home an extra $7000 this year? In the top tax bracket in Ontario, you'd need a raise of more than $14,000.

The tax tables in the Appendix following Chapter 15 will provide you with combined federal and provincial income tax rates, by province, so you can calculate the exact tax savings your 1999 RRSP contribution will yield. They will also help you decide if it makes more sense to work harder to earn more income or to concentrate on earning investment income—interest, capital gains, or dividends, in descending order of most heavily taxed.

Did you know . . .

. . . if you live in a province that is promising a tax cut next year, and you are in the top tax bracket, an RRSP contribution will be worth more to you in tax savings now than it will next year? So, it makes sense to catch up on missed contributions and to make your 2000 contribution now.

DON'T FORGET:

- Earned income is derived by working or from rental property; investment income cannot be included.
- For 2000, you can contribute 18% of your 1999 earned income, to a maximum of $13,500.
- Contributions to a company pension plan must be subtracted from your contribution room.
- Call Revenue Canada's TIPS line to determine how much room you have in missed contributions.
- Tax planning is an essential component in building your wealth.
- Your RRSP contribution refund is the same percentage as your tax bracket.

"I don't think anybody—from the upper to lower-income tax brackets—can afford to ignore the RRSP. It's a tax-saving measure, and it's an investment, and it's your retirement planning."

—Michele Wood-Tweedy, C.A., Principal,
Personal Advisory Services, KPMG

Chapter 5

From boring to the best: Get the right RRSP

Ho-hum RRSPs
Bottom line on GICs
Mutual fund RRSPs
Self-directed plans
Foreign content
Maximizing the 20%
Bending the rules
Splitting income

As you may recall, I mentioned earlier in this book that most people think an RRSP is a thing, a product—an investment on its own—and they believe that it always earns interest. Wrong. That is only the case when somebody—through choice or, usually, ignorance—decides to throw away the awesome flexibility and potential that RRSP rules allow, and have their money just sit in a no-risk, low-yield savings account or debt security like a guaranteed investment certificate, better known as a GIC.

These risk-averse folks want their money guaranteed, and rules have been put into place to do just that— ensuring nobody will lose their first $60,000 in a GIC issued by a bank, broker, trust, or credit union that's a member of the Canada Deposit Insurance Corporation.

The GIC-type RRSP is the preferred choice of most Canadians. And despite a drop in mutual fund sales at the end of the last RRSP season and a shift into guaranteed investment vehicles, people's thinking regarding their RRSP investments is nonetheless starting to change. It has to.

Our aging population is simply going to run out of private retirement funds if it relies on interest-bearing securities like savings accounts and GICs to build up their wealth. And this is certainly not appropriate for young people starting out on the investment path, or middle-aged people like me who have just 15 to 20 years left to maximize retirement assets.

In terms of RRSPs, you have three options—boring, better, and best. Similarly, you can assume one of three different levels of risk—none, some, and as much as you want. What route do you choose? Here's how they compare:

REALLY BORING ONES

At the bottom of the RRSP hierarchy are plans that put your money into either deposit accounts or GICs. Savings RRSPs pay a ridiculously low rate of interest that moves up and down with the prime, just like the rate you have on your daily interest chequing or savings account.

The advantages are that it is safe in the sense that the money on deposit will not go down. And you will be guaranteed up to $60,000 from Ottawa if your financial institution goes belly up.

But the overriding danger is that your savings will probably not even rise as much as inflation does, meaning you are actually suffering a loss in the purchasing power of your retirement nest egg.

It is my view that interest rates across the Western world will remain low for a long time to come—at least a decade—thanks to an aging population, low inflation, and declining government deficits. So, opening a savings RRSP should not be in the cards for most of us.

One step up (but only a small one) is the RRSP that puts your money in a GIC. It's still the most popular type, but the low rates of the 1990s are changing investment habits fast. So much so that financial institutions have had to come up with more zippy versions of this product—GICs tied to stock market performance. They do offer a somewhat better return, but more on that later in this chapter.

Source: David Brown, Toronto Star

A GIC works like this: You give the bank $5000 for five years and it agrees to pay you, say, 5% on that money in each of those years. Then the bank turns around, pools your $5000 with the investments of other people, and loans $50,000 out in the form of a five-year mortgage at 7%.

That's one way banks make money, and you earn 5%—guaranteed, just like the home owner is guaranteed that his or her mortgage rate will not rise over the same period.

So, a fixed rate is one advantage, and the GIC is again insured to the $60,000 limit. You know exactly how much money the investment will earn and, within an RRSP, the interest compounds tax-free.

But its advantages are also its drawbacks. In return for a fixed rate of return, the interest you earn will be as low as it goes. And in return for the time guarantee, you give up cashability and flexibility. The GIC cannot be cashed in and, if interest rates rise, you don't enjoy any of the increase. There is no potential for growth, or capital gain, and, as with a savings-type RRSP, your asset growth is not protected from the ravages of inflation, even the slight inflation that we have today.

These are all heavy prices to pay for the premium of no risk.

Did you know . . .

. . . there's a far better alternative to a GIC? It's a product that offers a greater rate of return and even less risk than a GIC, along with the potential for a capital gain and even the ability to cash it in before maturity. They are government strip bonds, and are issued by the federal and provincial governments, stripped of interest, so they are bought at a deep discount to face value. Principal is guaranteed by the government, no matter what the value, so there is no risk, and you can sell them at any time. Read the section "So, What Is a Government Strip Bond?" in Chapter 10.

THE LOWDOWN ON GICs

Because low interest rates have disillusioned a growing number of GIC fans, the banks have had to come up with new approaches.

Almost all of the new-wave GICs are marketed exclusively in the first couple of months of a new year—some others come out in the fall when the federal government is pushing its Canada Savings Bonds.

Frankly, most are gimmicks. Sure, you can improve by a little the rate of return you might enjoy on a regular GIC, but not by much. You are still better off, 10 times out of 10, investing in quality mainstream mutual funds or government bonds. But for many Canadians, life begins and ends with GICs, and for them even these small refinements are big news. Here are some of the newer GICs to look out for:

- **For those who think interest rates will be much lower in a year's time**—Extendible GICs. You lock your money up for a year, then have the right to extend the one-year rate for another year. Are rates going down? Likely not. So this is of dubious value.
- **For those who normally buy Canada Savings Bonds**—Redeemable GICs. On sale for a short period when CSBs are marketed, they are just like CSBs—cash them in after a few months and they'll pay a slightly higher rate of return. The advantages are the same as CSBs—a place to park cash for a while and earn more than in a bank savings account. For a long-term investment, forget it.
- **For those who wish interest rates would go up**—Escalating GICs. These give the appearance of high rates. Three years ago, for example,

Canada Trust brought out an escalating-rate GIC that went all the way to 10% after seven years. But here's the rub: The only true way to compare is to look at the blended rate—the average rate of return over all the years the GIC is locked in, which is very close to the traditional GIC rate. Sadly, you are taxed on the blended rate—taxes paid in the early years will be more than the return on your investment.

- **For people who want the sizzle of stock markets, but who are wimps**—Market index-related GICs. These increase the rate of return as stocks rise in value. Sounds good, but be careful. Many of these are just marketing creations and, in general, the premium you receive is tiny. The idea is to guarantee investors a minimum rate over a fixed period of time—usually a rate less than with traditional GICs of the same duration. Then you get extra if the TSE 300 or the TSE 35 index of the Standard and Poor's 500 index rises.

As a matter of fact . . .

. . . instead of purchasing stock-indexed GICs, you are far better off to invest in the stock market directly through equity-based mutual funds. These are professionally managed funds that spread investors' risk by investing in scores of stocks, in Canada, North America, or around the world. Not only will you benefit from the long-term growth of the stock market, but you will be paid income in the form of capital gains, not interest. So if the funds are ever held outside your RRSP, the income they generate will have much less tax exposure.

MUCH BETTER—MUTUAL FUND RRSPs

Mutual funds are growing so rapidly in popularity because they give most investors the double-digit rates of return they want, and need. Canadians now have more than $300 billion invested in mutual funds, while Americans have well over $3 trillion invested—about double our investment on a per capita basis.

All of the mutual fund companies can set up a mutual fund RRSP for you, or you can deal with your financial adviser. The hard part is deciding what kind of fund you want. There are almost 2000 to choose

Source: David Brown, Toronto Star

from, many in different categories. When asked how I pick my own mutual funds, my answer is always a surprise to most: I write out a cheque to my financial planner and tell him to pick. After all, he's the pro. So far, I have had no complaints. For example, my mutual funds went up last year, on average, 15.1%. I'm not greedy. That's enough.

If I were to pick my own funds, at my age (49), the obvious choice would be growth funds—those that are based on the performance of the stock market.

> ***Over the balance of the next 20 years, for many reasons (including falling interest rates, rising corporate profits, booming trade, low inflation, and the influence of the baby boomers) stock markets will boom. It is reasonable to expect your funds to double in value—tax-free within your RRSP—every five or six years.***

If you want less risk (although I believe that investing long term in the stock market is virtually free of risk), then you can put your money into fixed-income funds, which invest in bonds (government and corporate) as well as mortgages.

And if you can't decide, or want some growth as well as fixed-income security, there are balanced funds to consider. They spread their assets among both categories.

All of these funds will give you professional management and more diversification than you could ever get yourself. They have a vastly higher potential for growth than any kind of GIC but, of course, unlike a GIC, the returns are not guaranteed. There is more risk.

There is also usually more cost—most funds come with commissions attached, typically a few percentage points of the amount invested. Some funds charge the commission (called a "load") upfront when you buy it, while others charge you when fund units are cashed in.

The thought of paying a commission drives many people to invest in no-load funds like Altamira, T-D Green Line and other bank funds, or Scudder, to name a few. This is fine for people who want to save a few bucks, and many of the funds these companies manage have excellent track records. But, for me, it is really a false economy. Most no-load funds are also no-help funds. You do not get to access the expertise of a financial adviser to guide you into the right fund purchase.

Did you know . . .

. . . if you make a one-time investment of $2000 at age 22, you can amass about $200,000 by the time you hit 70? To do that, though, you have to average a return of about 10% a year—GICs and savings bonds won't get you there. If you have the earnings and drive to go for more, $2000 invested annually earning the same return for the same 48-year period will deliver more than $2 million.

SELF-DIRECTED RRSPs ARE BEST

Here is the way an RRSP should really work—the way you can take maximum advantage of all the strategies I am presenting in this book and that the rules currently allow.

A self-directed RRSP is nothing more than a bubble that shelters whatever is inside it from tax. It's not run by the bank, like a GIC

RRSP. And it's not run by a mutual fund company. Instead, it is run by you. But hopefully you have the wisdom to have it administered by a financial planner whose advice you trust.

It can cost between $100 and $300 a year in administration fees to a financial institution, or a broker, to run a self-directed RRSP. There are also some fees to pay when you transfer your existing RRSP assets into a self-directed plan. Still, this is a cheap way to get the flexibility and control needed to turbocharge your retirement assets.

Any qualifying investment can be put into a self-directed plan. You can buy and sell various assets and move them around within the bubble. The level of risk and the potential for growth are yours alone to determine.

But if you are working with a good adviser, and putting assets in the right places, like quality, equity-based mutual funds, the upside can be great.

You need only one self-directed plan. In fact, all of your tax-sheltered retirement assets should be consolidated within a single self-directed plan. That way they can be managed in harmony, and you will also keep administrative fees to a minimum.

How do you start a self-directed plan?

It's as simple as sitting down with your adviser, broker, or banker and filling out some forms. You can do this when you make your annual RRSP contribution; or you can open the plan and then transfer in either assets you already own (mutual funds, stocks, GICs, CSBs, etc.) or existing RRSPs at other institutions.

The transfer fee can cost as little as $25 or as much as $100, but don't fret about it. The advantages of having all your retirement assets in one plan will far outweigh the one-time transfer costs. Be aware, however, that transferring assets from an existing bank or trust can be a frustrating experience, taking weeks, even months.

> ***As these institutions are in fierce competition for your money, they are loathe to give it up. Notify them as early as possible that a maturing GIC or term deposit will be transferred. Then make sure you have a good paper trail.***

To do the transfer, fill out a T-2033 form (your broker, adviser, or banker has it) and have it sent to where the funds are. This will allow the funds to be sent to your self-directed plan without any taxes being deducted. If you don't do this, you could run the risk of your RRSP simply being collapsed, and therefore becoming fully taxable. Clearly, a bad idea.

Make arrangements to go to the bank to pick up a cashier's or certified cheque for the amount being transferred, then deliver it right away to where your self-directed plan is being administered.

Now, what do you put in your self-administered RRSP?

The answer depends on your age, assets, and tolerance for risk, the status of your spouse, and several other factors. In general, the younger you are, the more heavily invested you should be in stocks and equity mutual funds. As you age, the amount of fixed-income investments should rise.

And, as a general rule of thumb, your RRSP assets should be managed slightly more conservatively than assets you hold outside the plan. Why? Because their tax-free status simply means they will perform better, and you do not need to take as much risk to achieve the same rate of return.

Here's an example. As I write this, these are the asset summaries of my own self-directed RRSP:

GARTH TURNER'S ACCOUNTS

Self-directed RRSP	
Cash	0%
Fixed Income	35%
Mutual Funds	25%
Foreign Securities	40%
Total	100%

ADD SOME ZING WITH FOREIGN CONTENT

Canada is a great country, but you sure don't want to have all of your wealth in Canadian dollars.

Although the constant uncertainty surrounding Quebec has abated somewhat, our dollar could tank again when the separatist factions power up the referendum call to arms. History has shown us that the dollar falls, short-term interest rates spike higher, and financial assets melt every time the world starts hearing from the separatists. Foreign content provides a buffer during such events.

If you have all of your wealth in Canadian currency, you will lose purchasing power if interest rates rise—unless you have assets to offset that, assets that rise in value when the dollar falls. In other words, foreign assets, things denominated in other kinds of money.

Then there's the debt. For only the second time in Canadian history, federal government debt equals 100% of the country's total output. Yes, the first time was in 1946, after billions had been spent building the tanks and bombers that helped to win the Second World War. With the federal deficit eliminated, and many provinces also on the road to balanced or even surplus budgets, the picture has improved somewhat.

While that is reason to cheer, we still have a massive foreign debt obligation. In fact, we are so deeply in debt that the Department of Finance has admitted: "We have suffered a tangible loss of economic sovereignty."

The consequences for us as investors are stark. We are completely vulnerable to interest rate swings outside our borders and more susceptible to global financial gyrations than ever before.

Every 12 months, we ship almost $30 billion in Canadian currency out of the country and into the pockets of American, German, Japanese, and other bondholders in the form of interest.

This is fiscal insanity. It screams for political attention. But, to date, nobody in power in Ottawa has talked seriously about the need for laws to ensure that the federal budget stays balanced and the debt is tackled.

Now, you may not be able to change this, but you certainly can shield yourself from the debt disaster that is looming out there someplace beyond the year 2015. And your RRSP is the place to start.

Twenty percent of the assets in your RRSP can be held as foreign content. That is not nearly enough, but it's what we have to live with for now. Unless you invest in so-called "clone" funds (described below). Some of the largest mutual fund companies feel that raising the foreign content limit should be a major priority because the market's rapid growth is beginning to make it difficult to make appropriate investment choices at home in Canada.

This has been further complicated as the Canada Pension Plan starts investing those awfully high premiums into the markets as it tries to prepare for the growing number of new "clients" it expects over the next two decades. With all this new money going into the markets, the only outlet for this capitalization will have to be found outside of the country.

Also, the federal government has stopped new borrowing for the first time in 25 years. Three cheers. But this means that no new bonds will be issued—which will translate into a significant shortage of bonds for Canadian investors.

Despite these pressures, don't hold your breath and expect a move on the limits. Ottawa will still, and wrongly, dictate that most retirement money be invested in Canada—a rule not needed, and one that hurts investment in this country by signalling to foreigners that our markets require this measure of coddling.

> ***"If Canadians understand we're less than 3% of world market capitalization, then they will understand that the evolution of 30% will eventually happen."***
>
> *—Andrew Scipio del Campo, President and CEO, Scotia Securities Inc.*

Did you know . . .

. . . that Canadian investors who believe that the foreign content cap is too low have an average foreign content holding of only 16%? So says research conducted by the Bank of Nova Scotia. It also discovered that the average Canadian with an RRSP has only 9% foreign content in his or her plan, and 40% of Canadians have no foreign content at all.

So, by all means, do not restrict your foreign currency investments to what's in your RRSP. You can diversify outside your RRSP, as well as within it, in several ways:

- **Buy into global mutual funds**—They take your Canadian dollars and make investments denominated in foreign currency, while the fund unit price stays in Canadian currency. If the loonie falls, the relative worth of the foreign currency holdings rises, which buoys the fund unit price, protecting you.
- **Invest in Canadian companies giving you an income stream in other currencies**—For example, after the 1995 referendum, when it became clear that Lucien Bouchard would succeed Jacques Parizeau and become premier of Quebec, setting the stage for another referendum, I rebalanced my portfolio. One of my purchases was Royal Bank preferred shares, which paid me dividends in U.S. dollars.
- **If you want the security of fixed-income investments**—You can always buy government bonds denominated in other currencies. These bonds are issued by provincial governments or by Crown corporations like Ontario Hydro. They pay you interest in German marks or Japanese yen, and there is no need to convert your Canadian dollars into those currencies when you buy.

Source: David Brown, Toronto Star

Another new option—clone funds

Perhaps the biggest change in the mutual fund industry over the past couple of years has been the introduction of 100% RRSP-eligible versions of the fund companies' most popular foreign funds. These "clone" funds, as they are called throughout the finance sector, are set to flood the market and will provide much more exposure to foreign markets than your RRSP previously enjoyed.

However, they are not without drawbacks, namely their cost. Most add another 0.3% to 0.7% to the management expense ratio, which can translate into paying up to an extra 3% on the gains.

It's best to examine any venture into this area with your financial adviser and figure out how to work these products to your maximum advantage.

Maximizing the 20% zing

Up to 20% of the "book value" of your RRSP assets are allowed to be foreign—book value means the price you originally paid, not the market value, which is what the assets are worth today. The book value also includes all fees, loads, or commissions you had to pay to acquire those assets.

If your self-administered RRSP is managed by a professional financial adviser or broker (and it should be), then you will get a regular accounting of the percentage of foreign content. Just make sure it hovers around 19%, giving you a little flexibility.

If you are taking on the task of running your own RRSP, then here's what to remember:

- It's the book value that matters, not the market value. So if your global mutual funds rise in value, and all of a sudden amount to $3000 of your $10,000 RRSP, don't worry. Your book value has not changed.

- Revenue Canada will impose a penalty on your RRSP if the foreign content rises and stays above 20%. That penalty will be 1% a month on the excess—and it needs to be paid in precious RRSP-sheltered dollars.

  If this happens, then you must sell enough of the foreign assets to get back below the 20% limit, or deposit more assets into your plan (if you have contribution room available) to reduce the foreign assets to 20%, or swap the excess RRSP assets for non-foreign ones outside your RRSP. In the last case, you get to retain ownership of everything—you just rebalance your portfolio to stay within the rules (but be aware of the tax implications—cash will be subject to withholding tax and there is a potential for capital gains tax).

Source: Patrick Corrigan, Toronto Star

What constitutes foreign content?

Lots of things qualify. These include mortgages held on foreign properties or loaned to foreigners investing in Canada, limited partnerships (even if they are Canadian—because they already get favoured tax treatment), bonds issued by foreign governments (foreign-pay bonds issued by Canadian governments are not considered foreign content), and stocks of non-Canadian companies, even if they trade on Canadian stock exchanges.

But for most people, foreign content comes in just one form: mutual funds.

One example is global bond funds that invest in a basket of bonds from several countries. This reduces the risk to individual investors and counterbalances inevitable currency fluctuations.

But there are those who argue eloquently against "wasting" your valuable foreign content space on international bond funds. And it's an argument that makes sense: You can invest in the foreign-pay bonds of Canadian governments, Crown corporations, and corporations (as well as a few other institutions, like the World Bank) to get the same protection against the falling dollar as the foreign bond funds, but with-

CANADIAN UNDERACHIEVERS

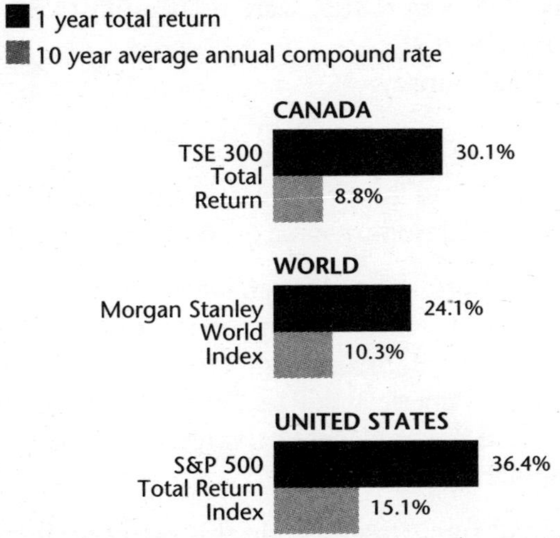

It doesn't always pay to be patriotic. Long-term investors have found better returns in foreign markets.

Source: Datastream, Morgan Stanley Capital International

out using any of your 20%. These funds are all considered to be Canadian content, even though they pay you in other currencies.

> ***So, this is probably the ultimate strategy: Use all your RRSP space for international equity funds—mutual funds that put their money into foreign stocks yielding you much higher long-term returns and more diversity of assets.***

There is no doubting the higher return most investors can get by going international. According to the Trust Company of the Bank of Montreal, over the last decade, people who invested in Canadian mutual funds earned a total return of about 75%, whereas investors in global funds have enjoyed cumulative returns of up to 500%.

In fact, the average compound rate of return of Canadian equity funds has been about 8%, while both American and international equity funds have yielded about 11%.

Meanwhile, all those Canadians afraid of losing any of their money (most people) earned a glorious 4% in their long-term GICs, which, even sheltered from tax within an RRSP, were reduced last year by inflation to a real return of about 2%.

That's not investing. That's lunacy.

How to exceed 20% foreign content

There are a few legal ways to boost the effective foreign content in your RRSP past 20%. And you should employ some or all of these strategies:

- First, as mentioned already, get as much of an income stream in foreign currency as you want by investing in foreign-pay Canadian bonds. Major governments and government agencies issue bonds that will pay you interest in American dollars, Swiss francs, or many other currencies. They are not considered foreign content and are completely RRSP eligible.

- There are several mutual funds that also do this—putting money into foreign-pay Canadian bonds, thereby making them RRSP eligible but not classifying them as foreign content.

- And speaking of mutual funds, you can also use Canadian funds to increase your foreign content. That's because many Canadian funds (including all Trimark funds) make sure they invest 20% of their cash in foreign assets. So, when you buy them, you are also upping your foreign exposure.

  Make sure you research the foreign content level of any Canadian mutual fund you are considering buying. The higher it is, the more you will be protected from fluctuations in the Canadian dollar.

- Invest in international financial institution bonds issued by outfits like the World Bank. Denominated in American and other currencies, they are RRSP eligible without using up foreign content room.

- And then, by holding the shares of a Canadian small business in your RRSP, you can jump your allowed foreign content up to 40%—double the regular limit. Ottawa will let you increase foreign content by three times the amount you have invested in that small business. The rules used to restrict small business shares to 50% of the value of your RRSP, but now there is no limit.

- Also, investing in "clone" funds can give you 100% foreign content, if you wish.

SPLIT INCOME WITH A SPOUSAL RRSP

Here's the typical drill for a lot of Canadian families: Dad works for four decades and ends up in the top tax bracket with a good pension or substantial RRSPs. Mom takes time out of the workforce to raise a family, has little retirement income, and has no personal savings. All of the family's liquid assets are in the hands of Dad, who pays the most tax.

There is something wrong, and costly, with this picture. For example, a retired couple in B.C. living on one income of $70,000 will see $22,000 evaporate in taxes. But if that one income could be split into two incomes of $35,000, the family tax savings would be almost $9000, because each spouse is then in a lower tax bracket.

If you need to be reminded how much $9000 a year is, consider this: To earn that much money after 40% tax, you'd have to have a five-year GIC yielding 6%, worth $250,000.

So, which is easier—finding an extra quarter of a million when you're retired, or making a few changes in your forties and fifties to shift assets into the hands of the less-taxed spouse?

Revenue Canada does not allow you to just give money to your spouse. It has rules—called attribution rules—that attribute earned or investment income back to you in most cases. One of the best ways around this is to contribute to a spousal RRSP. This simply means putting money into a plan that your sweetie owns; when he or she cashes the plan out, the money is taxed at your spouse's rate. If all works out well, that will be a rate lower than yours.

Now, before we talk about the mechanics of doing this, a special word of warning for everyone who is getting older. There is a growing bias in the Canadian tax system against seniors as Ottawa looks for money wherever it can find it.

The ill-advised Seniors Benefit is now history. But with the number of seniors tripling in the next 15 to 20 years, you can bet that Ottawa still views this group as a potential gold mine when it comes to finding new sources of revenue. After all, a number of aging boomers will have inherited a fair degree of wealth by that time, and many—if they've followed what I am suggesting in this book—will have assembled a considerable-sized nest egg.

Then there is the clawback of the Pension Income Credit and the Age Credit that adds a significant tax burden on higher-income earners.

Did you know . . .

. . . that the maximum amount of money available for investment by the Canada Pension Plan will be about a third less than originally estimated? Based on new projections, the maximum size of the CPP investment fund will be about $76 billion by year 2007. According to the 1998 budget, that amount was supposed to be in the $113-billion range.

Just about all of today's middle-class baby boomers, Generation Xers, and Echo Boomers will see no government cheques in their retirement years. Only the disabled and destitute will be cared for. The rest of us have to be smart as we prepare. And being smart means going spousal.

What's a spouse? Of course, the government has a definition (after all, what are governments for?). A spouse is "a person of the opposite sex to whom the individual is married or with whom the individual has cohabited in a conjugal relationship for a period of at least one year, or less than one year if the two individuals are the natural or adoptive parents of a child."

If you are gay or lesbian, there's a good chance this definition might be changed in the near future, allowing your partner to be legally considered a spouse. Now that Parliament has amended the Human Rights Act to outlaw discrimination against sexual orientation, it seems only a matter of time before the definition of spouse for tax purposes is also amended.

For the rest of us, here's how it works today:

- Once you find out how much you can contribute to your RRSP this year, you have a choice: Put it all in your own plan, put it all in a plan in your spouse's name, or split it between the two plans.

In other words, you can put as much as you want into a spousal RRSP, as long as it does not exceed your personal annual contribution limit.

- Of course, you can reduce your taxable income by the amount of the spousal RRSP contribution, just as with your own plan contributions.

- Your spousal contribution in no way affects your spouse's ability to contribute to his or her own plan, based on income. Just don't both of you contribute money to the same plan—the accounting is too complex when it comes to attribution for tax purposes. In fact, most banks and trusts won't even open up a joint RRSP for that reason.

- You can open a spousal plan at any place where a normal RRSP is offered—banks, trust companies, credit unions, brokers, financial planning firms, etc. It does not cost extra.
- When you open the spousal plan, make it clear that it's for your spouse and, as with all of your RRSPs, ensure that you name your spouse as beneficiary.
- Money has to stay in the spousal plan for three years before it is considered to be his or hers. After that time, your spouse can withdraw the money at any time, and it will be taxed at his or her rate. Take the money out before the three years are up and it is attributed right back to you, and taxed in your hands.
- But here's a twist: If you are the higher-income earner and consider yourself a candidate for downsizing, outsourcing, restructuring, or whatever other euphemism your company comes up with, then the attribution rule can work in your favour.

  If you are laid off, your spouse can withdraw money from his or her plan before three years have passed and it will be attributed back to you and taxed at your rate—which, when you are not employed, will be low.
- There is one circumstance under which spousal money can be taken out early with no attribution back to the contributor, and that's under the Home Buyers' Plan. Then you get to use it for a down payment and repay it within 15 years—with no tax and no interest.
- Besides helping you to effectively split income in retirement, thereby shaving your taxes, a spousal RRSP can also help avoid the clawback on the existing Old Age Security (OAS) and the Age Credit.

  If your income is more than $53,000, the clawback is 15% of the amount above $53,000 or your full OAS payment, whichever is less. So, by using a spousal RRSP, you can even out your two incomes and reduce the clawback. That means family income could be as high as $106,000 and both spouses would continue to receive the OAS. The same goes with the Age Credit, which is clawed back above an income of about $26,000. By splitting retirement income, a couple could earn $52,000, and both could still get the credit.

However, for anyone reading this book who is my age (49), or younger, you can pretty well forget about OAS, GIS, the Age Credit, and any other pension benefit Ottawa comes up with. These programs are luxuries that Canada will no longer be able to afford two decades from now. Let's face it—seniors are easy to tax. Their income streams are usually from fixed-income investments or pensions. That makes them sitting ducks for desperate governments. Your best hope is to split income, and make your duck as small as possible.

- Here's a good thing about a spousal RRSP: You can continue to put money into it, and get a break on your own taxes, no matter what age you are, so long as your sweetie is 69 or younger.
- And when your spouse arrives at age 69, the spousal RRSP can be converted into a RRIF, just like any other plan. The money that has to be withdrawn under RRIF rules will be taxed at your spouse's rate. Any amount more than that will be attributed back to you, if you have made a spousal plan contribution within the last three years.

Divorce, separation, or marital breakdown

And so we go from income splitting to just plain splitting. It happens. Frequently enough, in fact, that laws have been changed to deal quickly and decisively with retirement assets when the marriage or common-law relationship ends.

In this instance, a spousal RRSP is treated just the same as your own plan. While the money you put in your spouse's plan over the years legally belongs to him or her, when separation or divorce occurs, all retirement assets are deemed to be the property of both spouses, no matter who put in what—split 50-50.

Given that, there is no reason *not* to contribute to a spousal plan. If the marriage does last into retirement, you split the income stream and reduce taxes. If it does not last, the assets are treated exactly the same way. Obviously, staying married is better.

As with just about any RRSP, your spousal plan should be self-directed, giving you maximum flexibility to swap assets that are right for the times. And remember that, once set up, those assets belong to your spouse, not to you. Only he or she can take cash out, or authorize any activity within the plan.

WHAT YOU SHOULD DO:

- Examine closely stock index-linked GICs if you're leaning towards buying.
- Invest directly into the market via equity-based mutual funds; they beat the new GICs by far.
- Use one self-directed RRSP to protect your assets.
- Move any existing RRSPs and assets into the self-directed plan.
- Have your plan administered by a trusted financial adviser.
- When transferring a plan, stay on top of things; keep a clear paper trail.
- Have RRSP assets managed slightly more conservatively than those outside of your plan.
- Ensure that your RRSP has the maximum amount of foreign content allowed.
- Invest in Canadian companies that provide an income stream in other currencies.
- Buy government bonds denominated in other currencies if you want security of fixed income.
- Explore adding 100% RRSP-eligible versions or clones of popular foreign funds.
- Look for Canadian mutual funds that max out the foreign investment limit.
- Invest in international financial institution bonds that are RRSP eligible.
- Use a spousal RRSP to split income.

WHAT *NOT* TO DO:

- Try hard to avoid interest-bearing securities, especially low-interest GICs and savings bonds.
- Avoid savings RRSPs; they just won't do the trick.

- Don't use GICs or Canada Savings Bonds as long-term investments.
- Don't have all of your wealth in Canadian dollars.
- Don't be one of the 40% of Canadians with RRSPs who have no foreign content in their plans.
- Don't expect any government cheques during your retirement if you are younger than 50 right now.

"Retirement isn't the end of the road, just the start of a new stage. You should be thinking in terms of building your investments and generating sufficient income to maintain your accustomed lifestyle."
—John Platt, Vice President, Mutual Fund Research, Nesbitt Burns

Chapter 6

No cash? No problem. Potent RRSP strategies

You don't need cash
Moving tax-sheltered money
Carry on forward
Should you overcontribute?
No need to be timid
Asset allocation
From RRSP to RRIF

The RRSP bubble—such a simple instrument, and yet there sure are a lot of strategies, options, possibilities, and a tremendous amount of mind-numbing details to grasp, absorb, and put into action. That is why I constantly urge anyone with the least bit of interest in his or her financial future to make use of a qualified financial adviser. They know this stuff inside and out.

That is not to say that you shouldn't be tuned in to the ways that your RRSP can leverage your assets to ensure a sound financial picture once you take your gold watch and kiss the 9 to 5 routine goodbye. Familiarity with the many facets of RRSPs will help you productively discuss your needs with your financial planner, and ensure that the strategy developed works for you.

Here, for your consideration, are a few suggestions to make your RRSP the extremely potent financial tool that it is.

YOU DON'T NEED CASH TO CONTRIBUTE

Revenue Canada will pay you money to shelter assets you already own from tax. Honest. Here's why, and how.

Any financial security that qualifies to be in an RRSP can be put into a plan at any time, instead of cash. Assets you already own can be used as a contribution (up to your yearly limit), or you can transfer assets into your plan to use up the carry-forward on unused past contributions.

In return for doing that, the government will send you money—because the contribution of assets you already own will be treated the same way as a cash contribution would be. Revenue Canada calls this a "contribution in kind." I call it the excuse-breaker. With this rule in place, there is no excuse for just about anybody to miss an RRSP contribution, because almost all of us own something that could be dumped into this tax shelter.

A woman I worked with came to me some time ago with a simple question: Should she borrow money to make an RRSP contribution? Sure, I said, that makes sense. But maybe there's an even better strategy. And I asked her what assets she already had. It turned out she had $7000 in Canada Savings Bonds, purchased a few years back, paying 5.25%.

Because these bonds were not in an RRSP, and she was in the 41% tax bracket, the after-tax return was closer to 3%. And, after inflation of 1.5%, the real return was pathetic—almost not worth having the investment at all. So, we used the contribution-in-kind rule and a couple of other techniques to turn the $7000 into $39,000, and give her double-digit rates of return.

- First, she called her financial adviser and opened a self-directed RRSP. That cost just over $100.
- Then she transferred the CSBs into the plan, at a value slightly greater than $7000, because of accrued interest. Then she cashed them in.
- Then she went to the bank, got a $2800 RRSP loan at prime, and contributed that money to her plan, reaching her personal contribution level of just under $10,000. The bank waived repayment of the loan

Talk to him after the seminar! He's not standing, he's sitting on his wallet.

Source: Bob Kain, Toronto Star

until she got her tax refund (of $2870) for making the contribution in kind to her RRSP. And she used the refund to repay the loan.

- So, now she had about $10,000 in her self-directed RRSP, and was already way ahead of the game—more assets with the ability to grow free of tax.
- Then she used the money to buy a Province of Ontario strip bond maturing in 2010, with a maturity value of $39,000. She can hold the bond until then, and get all that money, or she can sell it at any time, if interest rates drop, and get a capital gain as the price of the bond rises. Either way, she wins.

The benefits here are obvious—a dramatic increase in assets and an investment with a good rate of return, shielded from tax.

As I hope you can see, money can be grown, without risk of any kind, using today's generous and flexible RRSP rules and a little investment common sense. But too many people don't understand the basics, thinking that an RRSP is not for them while they sit on taxable investments that could be both free of tax and leveraged much higher in value.

It's time to examine your own portfolio. Write down all the assets you own. If any of them qualify to go into a self-directed RRSP, and you have not made this year's contribution, or have unused contribution room from previous years, then call your financial adviser and make a contribution in kind.

CONTRIBUTIONS IN KIND

Qualifying securities	Yes, I own	Value
Canada Savings Bonds	________	________
Corporate bonds	________	________
Government bonds	________	________
GICs	________	________
Mutual-fund units	________	________
Limited Partnership units	________	________
Provincial savings bonds	________	________
Mortgages	________	________
Small business shares	________	________
Stocks	________	________
Term deposits	________	________
Strip bonds	________	________
Treasury bills	________	________
Cash	________	________
Cashable GICs	________	________

As you can see, many types of securities can be put into your RRSP in lieu of cash. Consider how much better off a middle-aged couple would be in retirement if every year they took a chunk of their portfolio and tax-sheltered it by making a contribution in kind, especially right into a spousal RRSP if one is in a lower tax bracket.

Some rules to remember:

- Start with a self-directed RRSP. Don't let this scare you—you don't need to administer it yourself, that's the job of your financial adviser. It will cost you $100 or so a year, which is money spent wisely. Never get talked into some low-paying GIC RRSP when you go to make an RRSP contribution.
- You can't make a contribution in kind larger than your annual RRSP limit plus any carry-forward room from previous years.
- The asset you contribute in kind has to be properly valued. If it's mutual fund units, then the market value on the day of transfer is the value, not the price you first paid for them. If it's a strip bond, the same applies. Canada Savings Bonds are credited to your RRSP for both the face value and compound interest.

- Revenue Canada rules stipulate that when the asset is transferred into your RRSP, it's the same as if it was sold. So if it has risen in value, you may have a tax liability. In the case of a stock or mutual fund, for example, that could generate a capital gain, which you must include in your taxable income for the year.

- However, if the asset has declined in value since you bought it, don't transfer it directly into your self-administered RRSP because you will not be able to claim a capital loss. Instead, sell the security, then use the cash to make the RRSP contribution. Now you can claim that capital loss against any capital gains.

- The rules also allow you to substitute assets you currently have inside your self-directed RRSP for assets you own on the outside—as long as they are qualifying assets. For example, if you needed cash and didn't want to borrow it from the bank, you could borrow it from your RRSP.

  That means you could transfer mutual fund units held outside the plan for assets inside it that could be converted to cash (Canada Savings Bonds, for example). So, you get the cash you need without having had to sell the funds—and you avoid triggering a capital gain.

- You can use the substitution rule to fine-tune your RRSP, to ensure you have the proper things inside it. For example, if you have any investments that pay you interest (GICs, for example) or that do not give you annual income but on which you still need to pay annual tax (like strip bonds), then they should be the first things stowed in the RRSP. Other investments, like stocks that pay you dividends, should be on the outside. That's because inside the RRSP you can't use the dividend tax credit, which saves tax.

  Substituting one asset for another doesn't affect your annual contribution limit but it doesn't earn a tax rebate. There is no restriction on how often you can swap assets, but some institutions will charge a fee.

- There is absolutely no guarantee that the contribution-in-kind rule won't be quashed in a future budget. Or, as mentioned earlier, there is also no guarantee that your ability to carry forward missed contributions won't be curtailed or even eliminated. Do these things now.

YOU CAN MOVE MONEY INSIDE PLANS

It's possible to move money between different RRSPs that you own, from an RRSP to a RRIF (Registered Retirement Income Fund), or vice versa, or from a pension plan to an RRSP, or vice versa. The rules are reasonable, but also complicated, and you should certainly get professional advice before doing this.

If you have various plans at several institutions, you should transfer them to one self-directed plan. That will give you the most options and flexibility. The transfer doesn't affect your annual contribution limit or get you a tax refund. But you do need to fill out the proper paperwork.

Your financial adviser, or the institution to which the transfer is being made, will handle it for you. Sometimes the place from where you are transferring will give you grief—imposing fees or penalties or delaying the move. Just stay on their case. And document every move.

- Money can move tax-free between an RRSP and a RRIF under certain circumstances. If you take too much money out of a RRIF, for example, you can transfer the excess back into an RRSP, if you are under 70 and have contribution room. Or, RRSP money can be used to set up a RRIF at any time. Of course, the only place that RRIF money can come from is an RRSP, an annuity, or another RRIF.
- A lump sum of money can be transferred from a registered pension plan into an RRSP, but it has to be done directly. You can't get the pension money and then put it into your RRSP without being dinged for tax.
- The same is true for transfers of retirement or severance packages (see Chapter 12). The money must go directly into your RRSP. Remember: If you accept payment in the form of a cheque, you'll lose up to 30% in taxes right off the top.
- And there are only a couple of instances when money can be transferred from your own RRSP into somebody else's—when your marriage goes bust or when you die, both of which can be unsettling all round.

In the instance of marital breakdown, the law requires that retirement assets be split evenly. That means RRSP money can be transferred directly into your ex-spouse's plan (or RRIF). For this to happen, you have to be living apart, and your significant other has to have met the definition of "spouse"—the opposite sex, married or common-law, or with whom you've had a child.

If you get back together again, the retirement assets may revert to your spouse's plan—which is an interesting form of income splitting.

> **Did you know . . .**
> . . . that stocks and stock funds, over the long term, have historically outperformed other investment classes? Between 1956 and 1996—from a boom time, followed by many years of economic turmoil, to the beginning of another boom time—the value of stocks, according to the TSE 300's average annual compound return, rose by 9.96% each year. That's almost 1.4% more than the annual average growth of bonds as measured by the ScotiaMcLeod Long Term Government Bond Index.

As for death, Revenue Canada deems this to be the equivalent of cashing in your RRSP or RRIF, and your estate has to pay tax on the whole amount—a good argument for spending all your money before you expire.

If you want to leave money for others, there are a couple of ways to do so. Easiest is simply making sure that all your retirement plans designate your spouse as beneficiary. After death, the assets will simply and quickly flow to him or her. It's worth checking now that you have done this in the proper place on your RRSP documents.

If your spouse has an RRSP, the money goes there free of tax. If he or she does not have an RRSP (and you don't want this to be the case), then the money is taxable.

And if there is no spouse, a child or grandchild may be designated, but only if nobody else has claimed a tax credit for that child, if the child's income was under $6456, or if he or she is physically or mentally disabled. In these cases, the assets can flow into an RRSP tax-free. Also, a dependent child under 18 can get funds tax-free to purchase an annuity until reaching 18.

Otherwise, the money can be used to purchase an annuity for the child, through a formula based on his or her age. This is an integral part of estate planning and the best advice I can give is this: Long before you give up the ghost, make sure you plan the disposition of your estate, and do this with a professional adviser.

YOU CAN CARRY UNUSED CONTRIBUTIONS FORWARD

Prior to March 1996, you were limited to seven years carry-forward. Now, there is no limit. This may sound like having your cake and eating it too—using your money now to pay down the mortgage, secure in the knowledge you can catch up on retirement savings later. But you'd be living a lie.

First, you lose all that tax-free compounding time for money you should have put into an RRSP—time that can never be regained in terms of growth. Second, if you keep putting off making your contributions, and suddenly the unlimited carry-forward provision is ended, that's gonna hurt. And then it may be almost impossible to ensure that you have sufficient money for retirement.

Already Canadians are vastly behind in savings contributions. Why are we leaving 80% or more of the allowable contributions (and huge tax savings) sitting on the table each year? There are several reasons:

- Following the recession in the 1990s, family finances are too tight for a retirement contribution.
- Canadians are generally unaware that, given cheap interest rates and rising financial markets, it makes perfect sense to borrow for their annual RRSP contributions.
- Not enough people are doing it the easy way—making monthly contributions through pre-authorized bank plans or payroll deductions.
- Canadians are generally ignorant of the fact that they can make a contribution in kind.
- The carry-forward rule gives a false sense of security, making it seem less urgent to contribute regularly.

Whatever the reason, this has helped create a very serious situation, in which Canadians are meeting only 20% or less of the goal. And that's exactly what the annual contribution limit is—the goal.

Did you know . . .

. . . RRSP limits do not come out of a hat? They have been carefully created by actuaries to meet assumptions about demographics, income needs, future economic conditions, and public pensions. Very few Canadians realize that.

The RRSP contribution limit is the recommended amount you should be putting away every year, without significantly altering your lifestyle. The assumption is that you will contribute for 35 years. So, if you're over 30 and don't have an RRSP, you're already behind.

Many people are staggeringly behind—well into their forties and early fifties with little, or nothing, saved. Together, Canadians have well over $200 billion in catching up to do. In fact, unused contributions from previous years account for over 70% of the total amount we can contribute this year.

Some people think that baby boomers, just entering their peak earning years, will make up a lot of lost ground in the next decade. Others point to the sizeable inheritances boomers will receive as their parents pass on. But I think both points are overstated.

Middle-aged baby boomers are, on average, way behind with their retirement savings, having socked away little more than $30,000 on average—in Canada, not enough to finance one year of retirement. Many simply will never be able to make up that lost ground. And as for inheritances, they are currently being spent by the longest-living and healthiest senior generation in North American history. In fact, many boomers will be hitting retirement with their parents still alive.

So, there is no easy or fast solution to the problem of the coming retirement crisis. Today's baby boomers should make use of their carry-forward immediately, and then get on a regular schedule of RRSP contributions, ideally monthly and by automatic withdrawal.

Here are some more strategies regarding the carry-forward provision:

- Younger taxpayers could concentrate on raising a family or paying down real estate, saving up unused RRSP contributions until they are in a higher tax bracket, and so earning a bigger refund.

  The danger here is that you won't get into the habit of making RRSP contributions, you are not building up savings that can compound, tax-free, for that extra period of time, and there is no guarantee that the government won't close the door on the ability to carry forward unused room.

- There's also the danger of building up carry-forward that you will never be able to use. It doesn't take many years of missed contributions to amass a great deal of unused contribution room.
- If you do gain an inheritance, be careful about how you use your carry-forward allowance. Dumping a great deal of money into an RRSP could temporarily drop you into a lower tax bracket, meaning a smaller refund. Or, it could make you subject to the alternative minimum tax, which was introduced in 1986 to make sure that wealthy people could not use deductions to reduce their taxable income to zero.
- Failing to make a regular annual contribution means losing the use of annual tax refunds. Remember, if you are in the 40% tax bracket, a $10,000 contribution earns you a $4000 cheque from Ottawa—money that can be reinvested in your retirement plan (using the carry-forward) or used to pay down an RRSP loan.
- But the most damaging aspect of postponing your RRSP contribution is the lost earnings that result from the tax-free compounding of assets.

So, here's the bottom line:

The carry-forward provision is a gift for those who have just discovered they are behind, and allowed to catch up. Make sure you *do* catch up. Borrow to do this, or use contributions in kind, putting the tax refund into your plan.

For those people who don't make a full contribution this year, figuring they will catch up later, be very aware of the danger in this strategy.

- ***The ability to carry forward unused contributions could end at any time.***
- ***The addition of each unused contribution just makes it that much harder to ever get all that money into your plan.***
- ***You are losing out on the greatest power of the RRSP—to allow assets to compound in value, tax-free, over a long period of time.***
- ***You are foregoing annual tax-rebate cheques that can increase your wealth.***
- ***You're gambling that you will be in a higher tax bracket later, when just the opposite could be the case.***

- ***And you are clearly falling behind. The annual contribution you are allowed make is the one you should make. Year after year for at least 35 years.***

YOU CAN MAKE AN OVERCONTRIBUTION

The law cuts you some slack by allowing your RRSP to have more money in it than the rules normally allow. It used to be a sizeable whack of money—up to $8000 in a cumulative lifetime overcontribution.

That was before the 1995 budget, when Ottawa chopped the $8000 right down to $2000. The penalty for having more than the allowed amount of money in your RRSP is a charge of 1% a month on the excess contribution, until you get rid of it. The penalty must be paid within three months of the end of the year in which you had the excess. Miss that deadline and Revenue Canada will also hit you with arrears.

As a matter of fact . . .

. . . if you're my age (50) and you overcontribute $2000 and manage to average 10% a year (not difficult with conservative, equity-based mutual funds), by age 68, it will have grown into $13,000. If you are fortunate enough to be 28 years old, and overcontribute the same amount at the same rate of return, when you're 68 it will have turned into more than $90,000! That's the power of tax-free compounding.

You can have that $2000 overcontribution living inside your plan for decades—and then use it as part of an annual contribution, getting a tax refund. So, who is ideally suited to use an overcontribution strategy?

- Obviously, young people. The younger the better, starting at 19, which is the minimum age for carrying an overcontribution. It makes sense for parents to make an overcontribution in the name of a child who does not have earned income and can't contribute to their own plan. There is no tax deduction, but by the time that child reaches the age of 59, he or she will be wealthier by about $90,000, thanks to your $2000 gift.
- Retired people who still have earned income (like rental income) can overcontribute, and then get the tax deduction back, even if their

RRSP has been converted into a RRIF. As long as you continue to have earned income, claim the deduction yearly at the rate of 18% of what you are earning—until the full $2000 is used up. The same thing goes for spousal RRSPs, as long as your spouse is 69 or younger. You can make an overcontribution, and then get the money back in deductions from your earned income.

- However, if you make the overcontribution before you retire, and don't have earned income, the money will be taxed twice. First, because you didn't get a refund when it went into the plan (it was already in after-tax dollars), and second, when it comes out of your RRIF as income, it's taxed again.
- Another reason to carry an overcontribution is to give a little personal protection in case you are unexpectedly laid off or incapacitated. Next year you might qualify to make an RRSP contribution (based on this year's earnings) but if you're out of work, it's unlikely you'd have the money. In that case, claim the $2000 overcontribution that you've been carrying as your RRSP contribution. That will earn you a refund cheque, just at a time you could use it.

Making an overcontribution makes perfect sense so long as you're careful to avoid going over the $2000 limit. The real purpose is to get as much money as possible into your plan for the longest possible period of time, at the highest rate of return.

So, if you do make an overcontribution, don't be content to have it sitting around growing at 4% or 5% in a GIC. Go for a growth mutual fund with the potential of doubling your money twice every decade.

THE CANADIAN PSYCHE: WE ARE RISK-CHALLENGED

Every year Canadians contribute just a fraction of what they could to their RRSPs, for reasons already discussed. What a tragedy. But, compounding the mistake, most of those who *do* contribute end up wimping out because they are afraid of taking a risk. They end up investing tax-sheltered retirement funds in GICs or savings bonds. Both, in my view, are a disaster and likely to remain so for the next decade.

Here's what I believe:

- The North American economy is growing and will continue to grow strongly, thanks to demographics.
- Inflation will be no real threat.
- Central banks want lower interest rates.
- GICs purchased today at low rates will probably come up for renewal at even lower rates.
- Aging baby boomers are about to gorge themselves on mutual funds, government bonds, and equities to get the double-digit returns they so badly need.
- This will accelerate the shift from real assets (like your house) to financial assets (stocks and mutual funds).
- Stock markets will continue to climb, albeit with corrections—sometimes massive—along the way. But, over time, there is no real risk in the stock market.
- We are all living extraordinarily long lives. If you are in your thirties or forties today, you could have more than 30 years of retirement to finance ahead of you.
- Government pensions are an endangered species. Don't count on one.

> ***If you share these beliefs, then it's obvious that the greatest threat we all face is outliving the pool of money we are amassing for decades of retirement. These economic fundamentals that are now in high gear demonstrate that the real risk is not losing money, it's not growing it fast enough.***

Too few Canadians realize this yet, so they continue to invest their RRSP money in the wrong places, and also opt for the wrong asset mix.

ALLOCATING YOUR ASSETS

Investing in your RRSP is important. Where your RRSP invests is even more important. You have three basic choices, or classes of assets. Each has a different level of risk and return associated with it:

Source: Financial Post

1. Cash equivalents—Low risk and low return. These are liquid investments that can be converted to cash quickly and on which it is impossible to actually lose money. Included are Canada Savings Bonds, provincial savings bonds, short-term bank deposits, and T-bill and money market mutual funds.

2. Fixed-income assets—Low to medium risk, low to moderate return. These pay you regular income at a fixed rate, but vary quite a bit in their flexibility. The three main contenders are GICs, bond or mortgage funds, and government bonds (not savings bonds):

- GICs are what most people opt for because they spell out how much money you will have upon maturity and they are insured against loss up to $60,000. They have some serious drawbacks, though: Interest rates are low, the money is locked up for years, and there's no potential for a capital gain.

I wouldn't put a nickel of RRSP money in a GIC.

- Bond and mortgage funds are mutual funds that invest in pools of government bonds or residential mortgages. They are attractive to people who want low risk and a predictable yield. Many investors do not realize that these funds are a terrible place to have money when interest rates rise, because they drop in value when that happens.

- Government bonds are a much better choice. You can buy regular government bonds that pay you interest on a periodic basis. Or (my favourite), strip bonds—bonds that have had the interest stripped from them, so they pay no income but are bought at a big discount to face value. The advantages over a GIC are extreme—they offer a better rate of interest, are cashable anytime, yield a capital gain if interest rates fall, and are 100% government guaranteed. See the section "So, What Is a Government Strip Bond?" in Chapter 10.

3. Growth assets—Higher risk, much higher return. These are assets that earn capital gains and appreciate much faster—but are also vulnerable to short-term declines. They are best for the buy-and-hold investor who realizes that building RRSP assets is a long-term project. The two you should concentrate on are:

- Equities, also known as stocks. You take on an equity, or ownership, position in a company when you buy its stock, or shares. These shares are traded in a variety of ways and constantly change in value according to the economy, the company's performance, and the laws of supply and demand. While the stock market has marched steadily higher over the last 100 years, not all stocks have gained, and there have been severe corrections that have lasted for years. Risk varies greatly—invest in bank stocks and receive steady, moderate growth, or pick a junior resource stock and get rich quick or, more likely, become destitute in a few months.

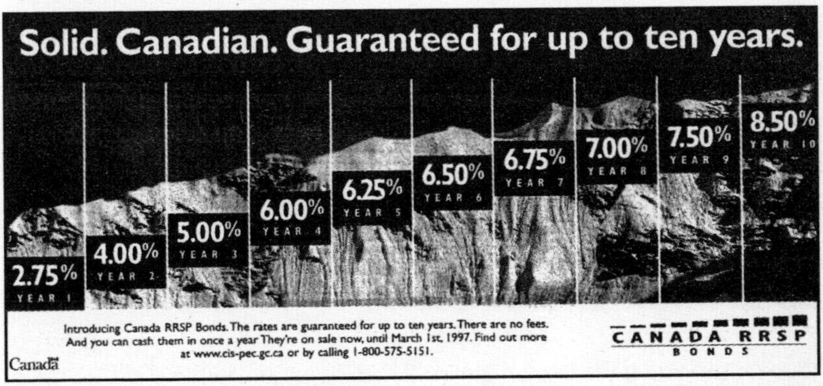

I can't imagine a much worse investment than Ottawa's RRSP bonds. This ties your money up for a decade for a 6% average yield. The price for taking no risk could be poverty.

- Mutual funds are pools of assets managed by professionals. Instead of trying to pick your own stocks you buy units in a fund that invests in dozens, or hundreds, of stocks. Mutual funds can invest in all kinds of things, and there are almost 2000 to choose from. It might seem like an impossible task to pick only four or six, which is why that's best left to your adviser. The important thing? Concentrate on long-term growth.

The further you are from retirement, the more money you should have in growth assets.

If you are in your twenties or thirties, there is nothing wrong with putting 100% of your retirement savings into high-octane, equity-based mutual funds. In your forties and fifties, having 60% in equity funds and the rest in fixed-income assets is still a conservative strategy.

And as for senior investors, they also need growth. The prevailing wisdom that seniors should invest only in fixed-income assets, especially GICs, is simply wrong. Anybody under the age of 80 should have some growth assets.

For the 10 essential rules of successful mutual fund investing, see my book *The Defence*. Any middle-aged person who is serious about financing his or her retirement has no option but to invest in mutual funds—now, and often. And stop being so Canadian, eh?

American families with mutual fund investments have, on average, $97,000 invested there. Canadian families with mutual funds have an average of just $42,000 invested. The Americans are twice as invested in funds as we are and, in my view, will build their wealth twice as quickly.

For the first time ever, Americans own more in mutual fund assets than they owe in consumer credit. Meanwhile, Canadian household debt is at an all-time high. We may be great savers, but we are only just starting to learn about investing. And we'd better learn fast.

LIFE AFTER RRSPs: CONVERT TO A RRIF

Okay, now you have been a good, if somewhat untraditional Canadian, have used all of the neat RRSP strategies, have saved and invested like a crazed beaver, and have built up a sizeable retirement nest egg. You are approaching age 69. What's next?

The rules say this is the end of your RRSP. You are no longer allowed to make contributions—now you have to start taking money out of it. That can be done in one of three ways:

Cash out and be taxed to the max

Option number one is to simply cash in all or part of your RRSPs by collapsing the plans. The result? A huge income tax hit—up to 30% will be withheld at source. So, why would anyone do this?

Well, before the government came to their senses and gave the Seniors Benefit the bum's rush, it would have made sense for some Canadians to cash out, take their tax hit early, and lower their tax profile. That way they could have reduced some of the double-taxation on most retirement income that the Seniors Benefit could have wrought. This is a moot point now. But, still, there are some Canadians who might feel it's best to take the money, pay the tax, and run.

> **Did you know . . .**
>
> . . . that about 56% of Canadians between ages 65 and 70 have RRSPs? When the rule change dropped the age of conversion to age 69, more than 400,000 individuals had to convert their RRSPs—up substantially from the previous year's 130,000. The Royal Bank reports that the average portfolio of its clients with maturing RRSPs is worth between $35,000 and $45,000.

Or, go for cash for life

The second option is to use the money in your RRSP to buy an annuity from an insurance company, bank, or trust. By giving over a lump sum of money, you get monthly cheques in return for as long as you live (a life annuity), or for a defined period of time (a fixed-term annuity).

The amount of money you receive will depend on your age, health, prevailing interest rates, and life expectancy. The younger and healthier you are, the less you receive. With a life annuity, the payments continue until you die, unless you have a joint and last survivor annuity, in which case payments continue until the last spouse expires. No payments are made into the estate or to beneficiaries.

With a fixed-term annuity, you usually get cheques until age 90, or you can base it on your spouse's age, if he or she is younger. Also

First there was the big 4-O; next the big 5-O; then 65, and now . . . life after RRSPs.

Source: Bob Kain, Toronto Star

available are "boutique" annuities, like ones indexed to inflation or a higher impaired annuity if you are in rough shape and likely to die sooner than the charts predict. And you can use non-RRSP money to purchase a prescribed annuity—which is a way of converting money in mutual funds or bonds, while leaving your RRSP assets to do what they really should do, and that is . . .

Best convert to a flexible RRIF

Consider a RRIF as a reverse RRSP, that is, you have to start taking money out. Contributions are no longer accepted. And after the first year, the amount you withdraw is determined by formula.

Of course, you pay tax on what's called the minimum annual payout (MAP). Taxes are not withheld by the bank or trust, like an RRSP, but the MAP is considered income and your marginal tax rate applies. So, for anyone with an income of over $60,000, you will lose half the amount withdrawn.

That's the bad news. The good news is that a RRIF is as flexible and generous as an RRSP in its ability to allow the assets in there to grow and compound free of tax. So, you should have your RRIF set up as a self-directed fund and follow the same growth strategies as you did with your RRSP.

Since RRIFs were created in 1978, the rules have been changed several times to make them more effective:

- You can have as many RRIFs as you want. But—like your RRSP—a single, big, self-directed one is best.
- The money no longer needs to be all taken out by age 90. Now a RRIF can be structured to give you income during your entire life.
- You can set up a RRIF at any age.

But the trade-off for this flexibility has been a higher required MAP in the early years of retirement. Here are the rules dictating how much money you have to withdraw.

Under the age of 69

Remember: You can set up a RRIF no matter what age you are, and the amount you must withdraw is less the younger you are. You are also allowed to have the minimum payments based on your spouse's age—which is great if you married young. Just make sure you choose that option when the RRIF is first set up.

Here's the formula:

$$\frac{\text{Value of your RRIF}}{\text{90 minus your age at beginning of year (or your spouse's)}} = \text{Minimum payment}$$

For example, if you are 65 and have $200,000 in your RRIF, then your minimum annual payment will be $200,000 divided by 90 minus 65 (which is 25), which equals $8000. If your spouse is 55, then the MAP is equal to $200,000 divided by 90 minus 55 (35), which equals $5714. Clearly, you are miles ahead in terms of deferring tax by having your spouse's age used instead of your own.

Over the age of 69

While the government dropped the age at which you have to convert your RRSP into a RRIF by two years to age 69, the formula for calculating minimum income stays the same until age 71—as described above.

After the age of 71, a specified percentage of your RRIF must be taken as income. There is no getting around this, but by using your younger spouse's age, the MAP can be reduced and more of your RRIF capital can be preserved to keep on growing tax-free inside the fund.

Each year a new calculation is made by your bank, trust company, or advisor to adjust the amount of income you must take in that year.

Here are the minimum payments, by age.

Age	Annual payment must be equal to this % of RRIF
71	7.38%
72	7.48
73	7.59
74	7.71
75	7.85
76	7.99
77	8.15
78	8.33
79	8.53
80	8.75
81	8.99
82	9.27
83	9.58
84	9.93
85	10.33
86	10.79
87	11.33
88	11.96
89	12.71
90	13.62
91	14.73
92	16.12
93	17.92
94 and over	20.00

You can see the tax bite grows steadily as you age, to the point when 20% of your assets have to be taken as income each year in your nineties. At that rate, the RRIF dwindles fast. But should you still be alive and kicking at that age, chances are your cash requirements will be very high—especially in the future, when more health care is privatized and the state can no longer afford subsidized institutional care.

That means a RRIF is important, but it should not be your only source of retirement income. So, past the age of 80 or so it would make sense to take a chunk of RRIF money and convert it to a life annuity.

That would bring down the minimum RRIF payments and give you an assured monthly cheque for life. But, there are other considerations if you are concerned about your estate.

When you cease to be a taxpayer

If there's any good news about dying, this may be it: Money in a RRIF gives you better estate protection than an annuity, which usually comes to an abrupt end when you do.

Always make it clear when you set up a RRIF who the beneficiary will be, and then back that up with a further declaration in your will. If you designate your spouse, then regular annual payouts can simply start flowing to him or her, or the spouse can collapse the plan, take all the money (and pay all the taxes), and go on a world cruise.

Alternatively, a younger spouse (under the age of 69) can roll the RRIF assets into his or her RRSP, or the RRIF can be collapsed and then restructured into a new RRIF according to the spouse's wishes.

And if you do not name a beneficiary at all, the RRIF is cashed in on your demise, with the money rolled into your estate and treated as income in that year. It's a good thing you won't be around to see that tax bill!

REMEMBER:

- Use assets you already own to maximize your contribution and unused RRSP room.
- There is no limit on the RRSP carry-forward room—use it before you lose it.
- Lots of carry-forward room? Borrow to fill it up, get a big tax refund, and let your investments compound.
- Make that overcontribution. But don't forget—it's only $2000, not $8000 any more.
- If you are in your thirties or forties, you could have to finance more than 30 years of retirement.
- Government bonds will always be a better choice than low-wattage GICs.

- Concentrate on long-term growth; tune out all the short-term noise.
- The further away from retirement you are, the more growth assets you should have.
- When you turn 69, you must convert your RRSP into a RRIF.
- Whether it's an RRSP or a RRIF, make it clear who the beneficiary will be on your demise.

"Canada has the lowest [inflation] rate in the G7 countries, a stunning performance in view of the strength of domestic growth and the decline of the Canadian dollar over the past year."

—Nesbitt Burns Inc., in its daily commentary

Chapter 7

Your house: A non-performing asset?

Mortgage versus RRSP
Equity—use it or lose it
Stock market myths

Interest rates took a big plunge in the second half of the 1990s, allowing many more people to achieve the great Canadian dream—buy a home, pay it off, and, upon retirement, have a tidy little nest egg equal to the home's value. For decades, most Canadians slavishly adhered to this strategy. Today, a great many Canadians still believe this is a sensible and workable approach.

Sorry. Today, that kind of thinking will get you nowhere fast. Despite the flurry of real estate activity over the past few years, the boom of the 1980s, just like rampant inflation, is not coming back. The values of many properties across the country still may never match their asking price 10 years ago, despite an improving housing market. Much of this recent boom can be attributed to pent-up demand being cut loose by the lowest interest rates in a generation and lots of first-time buyers.

Gen Xers, slowed down by the tough times in the early nineties, are finally making their way into the housing market—and this should keep the market buoyant for the next few years.

The baby boomers, who drove housing prices sky high in the seventies and eighties, are now content to sit on what they have, concentrate on amassing financial assets, and/or scale down a bit as the kids leave the nest.

> **As a matter of fact . . .**
> . . . real estate giant Royal Lepage says its research shows that only about 6% of individuals who come into an inheritance will use that transfer of wealth to buy a home. In the next 20 years, it is estimated that approximately $50 billion will be transferred annually via inheritances.

Despite the current activity, the long-term outlook for real estate is slower appreciation when compared to the past 40 or 50 years. Some niche markets will continue to do well—luxury condos, desirable neighbourhoods, prime cottage properties, and the like. However, the average Canadian home will not grow in value quite so quickly as most investment vehicles will.

Nevertheless, your home can still be a valuable asset. One, it can give a massive boost to the financial means you are going to need down the line, if you manage this resource properly. And two, you have to live somewhere. Today's low mortgage rates have actually made it cheaper to buy a home than to rent in any major city, with the exception of Vancouver—the most dangerous real estate market.

Here are some of my thoughts on the RRSP options available to home owners.

YOUR MORTGAGE VS. YOUR RRSP: NO CONTEST

Is it better to build up an RRSP or pay down a mortgage? Most financial advisers straddle the fence, saying that mortgage debt is expensive and non-deductible, and that the longer you have a home loan the more interest you pay. All very true. They also say the more years your money compounds tax-free within an RRSP, the greater the chances you will retire comfortably. Also a valid point.

And some advisers live by computer spreadsheets and formulae—to them it makes sense to pay down the mortgage first if the loan rate is 2% higher than what your RRSP investments are earning.

The final school of thought is this: Make your maximum RRSP contribution every year and use your tax refund to pay down the mortgage principal. This makes a lot of sense, and it will work. But it's slow. I have a better strategy rooted in the firm belief that residential real estate has no long-term future as an investment.

You should only be investing in residential real estate during the first half of your life, more as a forced-savings plan than as a way to build capital. In the second half of your life, sell or use the equity through leverage.

In my book *The Strategy* I detail why real estate, especially residential real estate, faces a steady, relentless erosion of value. The signs are all around us: The nineties have been cruel to home owners, reducing the net worth of millions of people through falling prices, rising maintenance costs, and vicious property taxes.

The average resale home price in the country's largest market, Toronto, hit $280,000 in the fall of 1989. It ranged lower by 31% to hit $193,000 in February 1996, before bouncing higher in the current real estate market. But it is a deceptive market, based on first-time buyers giving some scared baby boomers the chance to bail. The downward march will continue. At the very best, prices will stay the same.

Why is this? Because all over the industrialized world, especially in Canada with its rapidly aging population, the trend is away from real assets and towards financial assets—and real estate is a real asset.

The unfortunate part is that most Canadians have most of their wealth in the wrong type of assets—namely, in their homes.

The rise of financial assets in the coming decade—a trend that will explode in the first years of the new millennium—will only serve to drive real asset values lower. Already, with $3 trillion invested in mutual funds, American investors have shifted a large portion of what used to be home equity into stocks and bonds and other securities. This trend also had a spark lit under it two years ago when the U.S. government enacted a large capital gains tax break for individuals selling their homes.

> ***Demand for bricks and mortar will decline. That doesn't mean real estate is dead, but it is changing. Demographics will drastically shrink the number of potential buyers. Baby boomers hitting 50 after the year 2000 will start to become obsessed with the need to earn double-digit rates of return in their RRSPs, and will realize that they are sitting on tens or hundreds of thousands of dollars in their homes, which are earning them zero or even negative returns. Then it will be a race to see who can get out of residential real estate the fastest, before the value of some kinds of real estate—large, suburban homes, for example—simply evaporates.***

Why? Because there will not be the universe of buyers there to maintain those values. Here are some reasons why:

- Bummed out by uncertainty about their own employment prospects and the likelihood of an economic depression in the middle of their working lives, Generation Xers are in no mood to take on massive mortgage debt, like the baby boomers did in the eighties, when the charge was on to monster homes.
- Immigration has been a bright spot in markets like Vancouver, but many immigrant families tend to be larger and multigenerational, with the move to individual real estate much slower.
- And the baby boomers—all 9 million of them—generally are living in the largest homes of their lives, unlikely to move up and just about certain to move down.

So, why would you invest in real estate right now? Well, as a young person buying a starter home, it's a way to build up some equity in the kind of house that will have a better resale future—a townhouse, a condo, or a bungalow near services, which will appeal to aging boomers ten years from now.

Buying is also a way to stabilize housing costs, especially when mortgage rates are low. But for middle-aged and older people, real estate is a potential financial sinkhole. You should be getting at least some of your equity out and into the financial assets that have a gleaming future. Remember: You needn't sell your home—just don't have as much of your net worth in one vulnerable asset.

The strategy is this: Maximize your RRSP contribution, no matter what your age. Then, if you are a younger home owner, apply the tax refund to your mortgage and pay it off in the shortest possible time—but don't stop there. Use other techniques like weekly payments, which can shave more than a decade off the time it takes to retire a mortgage.

Younger investors can afford to take on a lot more risk than older ones. So, first-time home buyers who put money into RRSPs should be investing in growth assets—equity-based mutual funds, international growth funds, emerging market, Asian, and Latin American funds. Remember: Cash put into Fidelity Growth America Fund more than doubled in just five years; ditto for Investors U.S. Growth Fund, AIC Advantage, and other equity funds. And these are not considered to be the riskiest of funds, by any means.

As a matter of fact . . .

. . . $100,000 put into Templeton Growth 20 years ago grew into well over $2 million. And don't forget, during the past 20 years, Canada's economy has had to endure the effects of an oil crisis, two recessions, high interest rates, soaring inflation, numerous wars, the collapse of the Soviet empire, El Niño-related natural disasters, two major and several minor market corrections, Bre-X, the meltdown in the Far East, and a host of other calamities that temporarily influenced global markets.

Time is on the side of the young investor, and time always defeats risk. The further from retirement you are, the more valuable your RRSP contributions are because of tax-free compounding.

Will $100,000 equity in your house grow into $2 million two decades from now? Actually, I think you'll be lucky to get your money out with more than a small premium for inflation.

Always remember: Canadians have too much personal wealth tied up in their homes. The strategy worked most of the time since the Second World War—rising real estate values meant a lot of people didn't have to save and plan for retirement. Besides, "retirement" 20 years ago meant eight or 10 years. Now it can mean 30 years.

But as the new millennium begins, you must diversify your assets, shifting wealth until, approaching middle age, you have at least half of your net worth outside your home, then increase that amount as you near retirement.

> **Did you know . . .**
> . . . that almost 60% of Canadians who have paid off their mortgages don't have an RRSP? It's almost unforgivable.

And remember: Real estate is not liquid, meaning you can't cash it in unless you persuade somebody to buy it from you. Most people forget this, and end up selling at the wrong time, forced to sell by circumstances—and usually at a fire-sale price.

Or it can be the result of age and inaction—growing old, not doing what you should, and then being faced with a crisis when an illness strikes. I have experienced this firsthand in my own family, and I would not wish that on anyone. Real estate is not an appropriate asset for most seniors. It can end up destroying wealth—trapping it in bricks and mortar and eating it up in maintenance, insurance, taxes, and utilities.

Buy a house when you're young. Take the equity out and use it to build wealth when you are middle-aged. Dump it before you grow old.

After you are 40

Whether your house is paid for or not, take your RRSP refund and plow it back into financial assets. Because every year that passes, your assets have a shorter time to grow. You will be farther ahead to have them accumulate in your RRSP than to add to the equity in your home. After all, if real estate values decline between now and your retirement, the loss will not come off the mortgage—*that* stays constant. It will come off the equity in your home.

But if you do pay off your mortgage, make sure you keep writing monthly cheques of the same size—this time not to the bank or trust company, but to your RRSP. Take advantage of the financial discipline your mortgage gave you—set aside enough each month to meet an important obligation.

If you are in your thirties

Or, more probably, in your forties, and you have built up equity in your home, it's time to start using it. There are several ways of doing this, but one of the easiest is to call up the bank and get a home equity loan—a form of mortgage that will give you cash to invest. And why would you mortgage your home after having worked so hard to pay it off?

First, remember that residential real estate has no long-term future.

You do not want to be stuck with an expensive asset you can't sell unless you throw away a pile of equity. Ten or 15 years from now many Canadians will wake up to that reality.

Secondly, the interest you pay on a home equity loan is tax-deductible.

This is an investment loan. If you are in the 54% tax bracket, you simply write off 54% of the interest on your annual tax return. Of course, this dramatically lowers the actual cost of borrowing. Here's an example:

USING YOUR EQUITY

The true costs of a home equity loan used for investment purposes

Equity loan rate:	6%
Your tax rate:	54%
Rate write-off:	3.24%
Actual, after-tax loan rate:	2.76%

Where else could you find $50,000 or $100,000 with one phone call at an effective after-tax rate of just under 3%? By using your home equity and then investing the money in quality mutual funds that track stock market performance, you will suddenly see the money that used to be earning zero in your home suddenly making double-digit returns.

Source: The Globe and Mail

Is this a dangerous strategy? Some say yes. And when I first proffered this strategy in *2015: After the Boom*, there were critics and sceptics who had a hard time surrendering their eighties, inflationary notions that real estate is a secure and growing storehouse of wealth. Not to mention their irrational fear that the stock market is not the place where any careful Canadian invests.

That didn't surprise me. It's that kind of attitude that will keep many Canadians dependent in their old age on the dwindling crumbs of support offered by stretched-to-the-max government programs. They may be living in paid-up houses all right, but they also may have to choose between heating those houses or eating. That is why I devoted an entire book—*The Strategy*—to proper real estate investing.

THE DANGEROUS MYTH OF STOCK MARKET RISKS

History demonstrates that there is virtually no risk in the stock market as long as an investor is in it for the long haul and does not try to pick individual companies in which to invest. Those who will lose are the ones standing on the sidelines, their wealth parked in houses and GICs, wringing their hands and warning that one day the Dow Industrial Index could fall 1000 points, or maybe even 1500!

Of course it could, and possibly it will. But smart investors knew it was not the end of the world when just the equivalent happened on October 19, 1987—Black Monday. In hindsight, it turned out to be a heck of a buying opportunity, which is exactly what the next dump turned out to be 10 years later, almost to the exact day. Investors were a whole lot smarter that time. Not only did most hold their ground and not panic and sell, but the surge in market activity shortly after the correction demonstrated that a lot of bargain hunters were plunging back into the fray.

> ***Meanwhile, real estate has already seen its top. And it was an amazing coincidence that in 1987 the housing market peaked on about the same day that the stock market crashed. Or was it?***

BE AWARE THAT:

- Some real estate values may never recover to their 1980s highs.
- The long-term outlook for residential real estate is slower appreciation.
- Most residential real estate has no long-term future as an investment.
- Prices will probably decline; at best, they will remain the same.
- As real estate values decline, the loss comes off of the equity in your home, not off of the mortgage you owe.
- Your home can be a valuable asset if it is managed properly.
- Canadians have too much of their personal wealth tied up in their homes.
- At least half of your net worth should be in assets outside of your home.
- Residential real estate is not an appropriate asset for most seniors.
- Removing net worth from your home is as easy as getting a home equity loan for investment purposes.

"They [interest rates] may go up somewhat because the national economy is heating up a little bit, but they're never going to go up to the levels we had in the 1970s and 1980s when we had accumulating public debt and high inflation."

—Gordon Thiessen, Governor, Bank of Canada

Chapter 8

Another option: The RRSP mortgage

If you own a house, you can put your own mortgage inside your RRSP, and end up making mortgage payments to yourself. Working with a self-directed RRSP and the equity you've built up, you can actually transfer that equity into your tax-sheltered plan—and by doing so exceed the allowed contribution levels.

This is a bit tricky, and you need to follow the rules closely. This strategy only works if you already have an amount of cash (or cashable investments) in your RRSP equal to the mortgage currently on your home, or to the one you plan to place on it, to get the equity out. It will cost you a few thousand to set up and a few hundred a year in fees. But if you feel as I do—that the future belongs to liquid assets, not to real assets like housing—then this is a dramatic way for you to turn your house into a retirement plan.

First, the mechanics of setting up an RRSP mortgage, and then the equity strategy.

HOW AN RRSP MORTGAGE WORKS

Your RRSP is allowed to hold a mortgage on any Canadian real estate that you own—either residential or commercial—or on property owned by an immediate relative.

That means you can take money in your RRSP and loan it out as a mortgage. Then you must make regular payments back into your RRSP, just as you would with a bank mortgage.

One of the neat things about this is that you will end up paying far more back into your RRSP than you ever took out. In fact, this is the only way you can contribute more to your RRSP than is allowed under the regular contribution rules.

Because of the way mortgages are amortized, payments in the early years are almost all interest. Only in the final years do you actually begin paying the principal back. So over the course of a typical 25-year amortization, you will end up putting about three times more money into your RRSP than you took out of it.

Did you know . . .

. . . that most Canadians have the bulk of their financial assets tied up in non-liquid assets such as their homes and GICs? With low inflation, and with few exceptions, most house prices will not appreciate. And with interest rates likely to remain low for years to come, GIC returns will maintain their pitiful earning power, or lack of it.

In the meantime, you can use the payments made into your RRSP to invest in growth mutual funds to get solid double-digit returns. So, the idea here is completely opposite to a conventional mortgage—which you want to pay off as fast as possible. The goal with an RRSP mortgage is to make it last as long as you can and to be as costly as possible, so you can maximize the transfer of wealth into the retirement plan.

There are several ways of doing this.

- First, go with the longest amortization period possible. The longer it takes you to pay it off, the more interest accrues and the greater the amount of money going into the RRSP.
- Second, the government stipulates that your RRSP mortgage interest rate must be "comparable" to market rates. Shop around, find the highest rate offered commercially, and use that as your RRSP mortgage rate.
- Third, make your RRSP mortgage an open one, which would allow you to pay it off at any time (which you have no intention of doing). Open mortgages cost a premium rate, meaning your interest is greater.
- Fourth, you can make the mortgage a second one, to boost the interest rate even higher. (But this will also cost you more in mortgage insurance—all RRSP mortgages have to be insured by CMHC or GE Capital—the only two insurers currently available.)
- Finally, stay away from all the techniques that people normally use to accelerate repayment of mortgages. In other words, you want a monthly-pay mortgage, instead of a weekly one that cuts repayment time and saves a lot in interest. You don't want to pay less into your RRSP; you want to pay as much as possible!

An RRSP mortgage has the same flexibility and constraints as a bank mortgage. You can choose any length of term that is commercially available, and if you default on your payments, your RRSP ends up taking ownership of your home—which you don't want.

RRSPs are allowed to finance real estate, not own it, so your plan would be required to sell the home within a year, at market value.

There are certainly expensive set-up costs and moderate maintenance costs involved and, as mentioned, this has to be done through a self-directed retirement plan. But it's still worth it. Here's the procedure:

- Costs include an appraisal fee (typically $150 to $200), legal fees ($500 or more), and a one-time set-up fee (anywhere from $100 to $300, depending on the financial institution). Also, all RRSP mortgages have to be insured, generally costing about 2% of the mortgage amount, or $2000 on a $100,000 loan. Normally you'd pay this in cash rather than adding it to the mortgage principal, because by tacking it on, it also gets amortized and ends up costing you three times what you borrowed. But in this instance, because the goal is to get money into your RRSP, you gladly add it to the outstanding debt.

- Once in place, the RRSP mortgage has some ongoing costs. The annual fee for the self-directed plan is typically $150 and then there is a mortgage administration fee that varies, from less than $100 to almost $300 annually. Revenue Canada stipulates that you can't administer your own RRSP mortgage—you'll need a third-party agent, typically a trust company.
- Not all financial institutions will allow you to have an RRSP mortgage within a self-directed plan. Others will only allow it on your principal residence. Still others are completely flexible—so shop around.
- As stated, you need to have enough cash or cashable assets in your RRSP to equal the mortgage you are transferring to your plan. If your RRSP assets are locked in to GICs, for example, it won't work. And once the RRSP mortgage is set up, it's locked in until the time of renewal, when you have some options.

USING AN RRSP MORTGAGE TO GET EQUITY OUT OF YOUR HOME

In most cases where people have existing mortgages on their homes and less than $50,000 cash in their RRSP, it does not make sense to set up an RRSP mortgage. Initial and ongoing costs are too high to compete with the return your money could get elsewhere. But there are some circumstances under which this strategy allows you to get equity out of real estate and at the same time exceed the RRSP contribution levels. Is this you?

- You own your home, mortgage-free, which means you have a significant amount of equity (probably growing at a rate less than most conservative investments in Canada; depending on where you live, earnings on that equity could be flat or declining),
- You have a whack of cash or cashable assets (CSBs, strip bonds, mutual funds, etc.) in your RRSP, and,
- You have a good cash flow that you'd like to divert into your RRSP.

Here's a plan for somebody with $150,000 equity in their home, and an equal amount in RRSP assets, invested in a 6% five-year GIC (the typical Canadian strategy):

(1) Take out a home equity loan for $150,000—You can do this easily through a financial institution, or most full-service financial advisers will set it up for you, sometimes even free of charge.

(2) Invest that money in, say, equity-based mutual funds to earn at least 10%—Now your home equity loan is deemed to be an investment loan for tax purposes.

(3) As such, the interest on the equity loan is tax-deductible—So, if you are in the 54% tax bracket, at income tax time, deduct 54% of the interest you paid all year. Your taxable income will drop as a result.

(4) Now, set up an RRSP mortgage—This will allow your retirement plan to buy out the bank or trust company mortgage. You can insure this through GE Capital or, if you have waited up to a year after taking the equity loan, CMHC will insure the mortgage (CMHC has a rule against insuring equity loans, but after a period of time in existence it becomes a normal mortgage).

Okay, let's review: You have taken $150,000 out of the equity in your home and it is now earning you at least 10% (instead of zero). At the same time, you have created a tax deduction and reduced your income tax load. And now your RRSP holds a $150,000 mortgage, instead of the assets that used to be there.

(5) Now, every month, cut a cheque to your RRSP in the form of a mortgage payment—At a five-year rate of around 7% that monthly cheque would be more than $1200. And so, each year, you would be contributing almost $15,000 to your RRSP. That's about $1500 more than the current maximum limit of $13,500, and it doesn't matter what your income level is. To make the maximum $13,500 payment, you'd have to be earning more than $75,000. But with an RRSP mortgage you could be contributing about $15,000 while making just $60,000, which normally would mean a maximum contribution of only $10,800.

(6) In five years, you will be able to contribute about $75,000 to your RRSP—During that time, if you put that money into growth-oriented mutual funds averaging 10% (and you should do much better than that), your RRSP will have close to $100,000 returned to it.

The bottom line is increased wealth. Five years after having $150,000 equity in your home and $150,000 in your RRSP (which would have grown to just over $200,000), you'd have a total of $350,000. Instead, now you would have a $150,000 mortgage in your RRSP, about $100,000 in new RRSP assets, and over $200,000 in outside investments (assuming that the $150,000 grew by about 12 to 13% after capital gains tax)—for a total of around $450,000.

If you had not arranged the equity loan and then the RRSP mortgage, the $150,000 in your RRSP would certainly have continued to grow, but the equity in your home likely would not have grown and perhaps even would have shrunk. And you would not have had the mortgage interest to help reduce your taxable income.

With such things possible, isn't it amazing that most people continue to sit on all that money in their homes?

THE HOME BUYERS' PLAN: BUYER BEWARE

RRSP mortgages are a great way for people with equity to get money out of their homes and to increase their RRSP contributions. In contrast, the Home Buyers' Plan is geared to first-time buyers. As an MP, I lobbied for this plan to come into effect, and let me tell you why.

In 1991, during the depths of the recession, the residential construction sector was suffering terribly and the Canadian Real Estate Association (CREA) came up with the idea of letting people temporarily borrow from their RRSPs to buy a home. I told CREA that I would help their cause and, along with other supportive MPs, we convinced Finance Minister Don Mazankowski to give it a shot. He did so in the 1992 budget.

The response was unreal—within a year almost a quarter of a million people borrowed more than $2 billion to finance houses. Originally the program was to end in early 1994, but current Finance Minister Paul Martin surprised a lot of people by making it permanent. And now I have second thoughts about it.

The plan did what it was intended to do—it gave a shot of adrenalin to the housing market when it was really needed. At the time, those against it argued that the measure corrupted the whole intent of the RRSP system, which was to encourage people to put money away for retirement.

While I realize that the Home Buyers' Plan is still popular, and supported by the real estate industry, the critics' arguments got a lot stronger and more valid when the plan was carved in stone. And, yes, there are dangers inherit in using this plan, unless you know how to work it, and what to do once it is in effect.

How it works

You can withdraw up to $20,000 from existing funds in your RRSP to buy a home. If you have a spouse, together you can withdraw up to $40,000. The plan is open only to first-time buyers. You must be a Canadian resident with an RRSP who has not used this plan before and has not owned a home in the last five years, or you must be married to or living with someone (of the opposite sex) who has not owned a home for five years.

The money has to be used to buy an existing or to-be-built house by October 1 of the year following the withdrawal. It can be a condo, detached home, mobile trailer, apartment unit in a duplex or triplex, cooperative, or townhouse. The money can't be used to pay down an existing mortgage or to fix up a house you already own. To apply for the Home Buyers' Plan, simply fill out the right form at your bank or trust company and then you can withdraw the money from your RRSP and no taxes will be withheld.

In effect, you are taking an interest-free loan from your RRSP, which you will have to pay back. Miss a repayment, and it becomes part of your income for that year, and that means you pay tax on it, and lose the ability to put it back into your RRSP.

How you repay the interest-free loan

You must repay the money within 15 years of taking it out of your RRSP—in equal payments. So the maximum $20,000 interest-free and tax-free loan would have to be repaid in annual instalments of $1333. The repayments start in the second calendar year after you borrow, giving new home buyers time to get their financial house in order. So, a loan taken out in 2000 under the Home Buyers' Plan will need repayments beginning in 2002.

But even that can be delayed. Repayment rules were changed to the RRSP contribution deadline—60 days into the next year. So, borrow in 2000 and your first payment is due March 1, 2003.

Repayments do not have to be made into the same RRSP they came out of but, of course, you can't claim a tax deduction when you make a repayment—you already got that when the money first went into your plan.

Revenue Canada will send you a borrower's notification form that gives an annual statement; watch for it—it will tell you exactly how much is due, and by when. It also includes a summary of the payments you've already made. You can always pay back more than required, but not less. And when you do make an overpayment, future payments will be scaled back to reflect that.

If you are turning 69 and your plan isn't paid back, you can pay it out in full if you have the money, or include it in your income each year, and spread out the tax liability.

A neat strategy to use

If you are planning to buy a home, and you don't have an RRSP, try to make the closing date on the real estate transaction 90 days or more from the time of signing the offer. This is because you can make an RRSP contribution and take out a tax-free, interest-free loan under the Home Buyers' Plan in the same year. The two actions just have to be at least 90 days apart.

First, go to the bank, trust, or personal adviser and open an RRSP, putting in $20,000 from your down payment savings, if you have the accumulated RRSP room. That will earn you a tax rebate cheque from the government of $8000 if you're in the 40% tax bracket.

Then, on closing 90 days later, use the Home Buyers' Plan to withdraw the $20,000 without penalty. You have just increased your wealth by $8000 in three months, for a few minutes' work filling out two forms. For first-time home buyers, $8000 can sure come in handy down the road for appliances, decorating, furniture, or, better still, reducing the mortgage principal.

But the plan can also be dangerous

As I said above, the point of RRSPs is to encourage people to save for their retirement. The Home Buyers' Plan was intended to be a temporary stimulus to a comatose real estate industry. But since it has become permanent, it represents a serious precedent for using the $150 billion pot of RRSP funds for things that have nothing to do with retirement.

For somebody taking money out of their RRSP to buy a home, consider this: There is no way the value of that house is going to grow enough in the next three decades to compensate for the lost power of that $20,000 (or whatever amount is borrowed) growing tax-free within your RRSP. And the younger you are, the more money you will lose. Ironically, the bulk of the people using the Home Buyers' Plan are younger, first-time buyers—the people for whom this plan is the most dangerous.

Did you know . . .

. . . that $20,000 taken out of an RRSP in your twenties can represent $200,000 lost when you are in your sixties? Will your home rise ten times in value between now and 2037? I seriously doubt it. If it paces inflation, you'll be doing well.

So, think hard and long before you remove RRSP money for a down payment. If you decide to borrow from your RRSP, pay it back into your plan as fast as possible—don't spread it out over a long decade and a half. And certainly keep putting money into an RRSP after you buy the house. Get on a monthly contribution plan. Just think of your monthly RRSP contributions as a payback on the money you saved reducing the mortgage by the amount of your Home Buyers' Plan loan.

KEEP THIS IN MIND:

- Your RRSP can hold your mortgage.
- You must have cash or cashable assets in your RRSP equal to the mortgage.
- Because of associated cost, this strategy works best for amounts substantially above $50,000.
- You can end up putting more into your RRSP than you took out of it.
- You can exceed contribution limits by holding an RRSP mortgage.

- First-time home buyers can tap their RRSP for an interest-free loan—up to $20,000.
- If you have a spouse, together you can take out a tax-free loan for up to $40,000.
- Repayment—in equal instalments—must be made within 15 years of taking out the loan.
- You are losing the tax-free compounding of that money during the time it is out of your RRSP.

"An RRSP is a financial cornerstone, it's easy to get started and maintain. But for homeowners, their property is a huge asset in their total portfolio. It should get a lot of attention in the overall plan, so it does not become a liability in retirement, or before."

—Robert Frances, President, PEAK Financial Group

Chapter 9

The top ten: Strategies you can't afford to ignore

Invest for growth
Catch up now
Contribute early
Maximize cash flow
Spousal RRSPs
The overcontribution
An interest-free loan
Contribute in kind
RRSP mortgage
Free up real estate

There is no doubt in my mind that as we enter the new millennium this is a critical time for most Canadians. While the economy and financial markets have made fantastic strides since the recession of the early nineties—and we're poised for even more growth over the next decade or so—most people don't see it and are not investing to take advantage of what will come. Record numbers of Canadians have been cashing in their RRSPs, and a staggering 50% of them are baby boomers—under the age of 55.

There is nothing weak about the economy. In fact, the economic future is very bright. The problem is that Canadians are investing in the wrong ways, and in the wrong places. Too few are taking advantage of today's outstanding opportunities because they fear the future. Worse, they are not harnessing the power of the RRSP.

Study the strategies I am presenting here and elsewhere in this book. Discuss them with your financial adviser. If you don't have an adviser, then get one. Finally, do what most Canadians will not—take action, and implement these strategies. Never, never assume that in the years to come the government will be there to support you, or that future investments will make up for lost ground today. That just won't happen.

As I write this, most at risk are the baby boomers, who now must earn double-digit rates of return within their RRSPs for the next dozen or so years if they harbour a hope of maintaining a middle-class lifestyle in retirement. Most are not doing it, still wedded to the twin myths that:

(a) retirement assets should be held in risk-free investments like GICs, and

(b) money plowed into real estate is safe.

Individuals who do not quickly shake those beliefs will end up both bitter and poorer. Don't be one of them. So, are you ready? Then let's begin . . .

1. GO FOR GROWTH

RRSPs are not GICs. RRSPs are merely mechanisms for shielding your assets from tax. That means they are ideal for harbouring highly taxed assets like strip bonds. For example, a government bond paying 8% held for 30 years within an RRSP would give you double the return on the same bond held outside the plan—even assuming you paid the top marginal tax rate when you cashed out the RRSP.

In fact, an RRSP is so effective at maximizing the yield on such an investment that—according to the calculations of Bruce Cohen of the

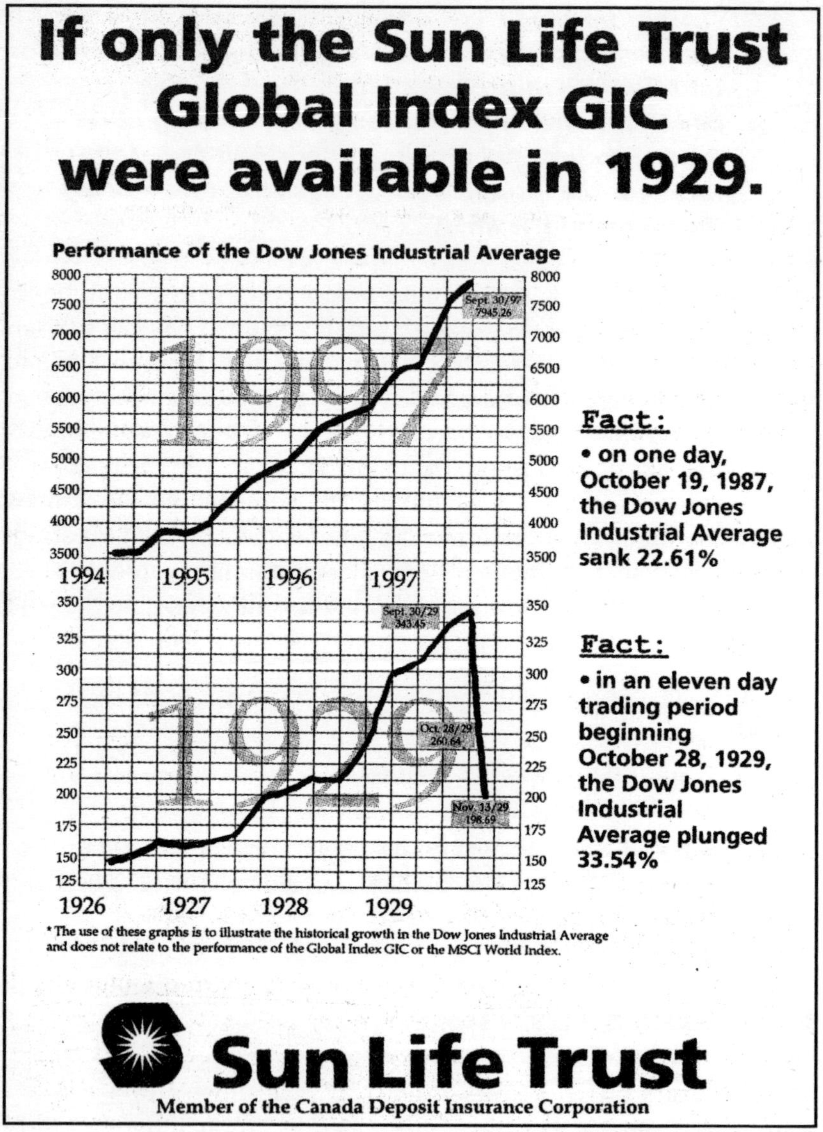

Market volatility—a regular feature of stock market activity (the 1929 crash being a total aberration)—is frequently exploited by the media and financial institutions' marketing departments and ad agencies. Despite the occasional plunge, the stock market continues to provide excellent returns for astute and prudent long-term investors.

Financial Post—future tax rates could soar as high as 82% and you'd still be better off having money in an RRSP cashed out at that tax level.

Rule One: Assets that are most susceptible to tax should go into your RRSP first.

That includes strip bonds, savings bonds, mortgages, and GICs. And remember: Strip bonds always beat GICs, because you get a better rate of return with less risk, plus the ability to cash out at any time.

Growth investments, even with a lower tax profile than bonds and investment certificates, also belong in your RRSP. If you are a baby boomer or younger, it is essential to have growth-oriented assets in your plan. And the best growth assets to have are stocks and mutual funds. How can you go wrong, for example, by buying shares in major Canadian banks? These companies are wildly profitable with a stranglehold on the financial services sector and a virtual monopoly on the domestic market, and they are growing globally, too.

And, of course, quality, equity-based mutual funds have been giving investors double-digit returns through most of the 1990s.

There is little reason to believe this won't continue, and much to suggest that the golden age of equities is nicely under way—swollen by a river of money flowing out of low-yielding, fixed-income investments, real estate equity that has been delivering zero rates of return, and the savings of the boomers who are growing desperate for high numbers.

In February 1997, Canadians put more money into mutual funds than during any other month in Canadian history. And yet just one year later, the 1998 RRSP season showed that there are still a lot of nervous Nellies afraid of risk who still do not realize that their fears are putting their futures in jeopardy. Net sales of funds in January 1998 were down 36% from a year earlier to $3.4 billion, while February 1998 sales were down 25% to $7.9 billion. As for 1999, some of the hesitancy and nervousness still persisted.

Some people worry that so much money is on the move that another huge stock market correction is imminent and we could head into a major 1929-style depression. That was the message the late Andy Sarlos offered up in his 1996 book, *Fear, Greed and the End of the Rainbow.*

But with an aging North American population, the need for high rates of return will likely keep most investors in the market and even increasing their holdings when prices take the inevitable tumble.

Make sure you grab some of this growth. I fail to see the risk in buying and holding quality funds like Templeton Growth, Fidelity Growth America, Trimark, Investors U.S. Growth, C.I. Canadian Growth, or many others. The key here is to make sure you are a long-term investor, buying these funds and holding them for a minimum of five years. Fifteen years would be even better.

> ***I believe there is virtually no downside to the stock market, as long as an investment is held long enough.***

As a matter of fact . . .

. . . if you take a look at any chart of the stock market over 15, 40, or 100 years, you can clearly see that the trend for prices is higher. The smart money buys on weakness and only sells on necessity, not panic.

Over the last three decades, the Toronto Stock Exchange has yielded an average return of almost 10%—beating out every other asset class. And now with low inflation and reasonably low interest rates, equities will attract more interest and the pressure for higher prices will increase. Can you afford not to invest?

2. MAKE THOSE MISSED CONTRIBUTIONS—NOW

Considering that the RRSP is the best tax shelter in North America, it is shocking that less than a third of Canadians who file tax returns make an RRSP contribution. Only 11% make their maximum contributions.

Millions of people in this country have savings, but they are not tax-sheltered in an RRSP. These people pay far more tax than they need to, and are not enjoying full compounding of their investments. Others do not realize that contributing just $100 a month to a plan can result in a

Source: Duffy, Toronto Sun

quarter-million dollar RRSP in 25 years. Total unused contribution room is growing by leaps and bounds and is nearing the point at which the build-up is so huge it may never be realized.

And there is no reason to believe that this huge amount of contribution room exists because people don't know any better. According to a study published by the Bank of Nova Scotia, 87% of Canadians know they can make up missed contributions. Equally disturbing: More than half of those surveyed hadn't a clue how much room they had to work with, or where they could get this information. This kind of lackadaisical attitude towards financial planning has got to change.

And as I argue elsewhere in this book, there is reason to believe that the current ability to catch up on missed contributions will be ended at some point. Because if everyone were to do what I am suggesting, there is no doubt we would have a new federal deficit exploding on Parliament Hill. Ottawa's goal of maintaining a balanced budget (no operating deficit) would be totally sabotaged. And that is why one of these next few budgets will clearly signal that lost contributions will stay lost.

That means it is imperative to catch up now, while you still have the opportunity. If you are reading this book during "RRSP season"

2000—those few weeks of the year prior to the beginning of March—then this is what I want you to do:

1. Make your full 1999 contribution, then

2. Make the allowable overcontribution of $2000

3. Catch up on all of your missed past contributions.

You can find out the amount of missed past contributions in one of two ways. First, get your financial adviser to do it for you because that's part of the normal job he or she should be doing. Or, you can call Revenue Canada and find out yourself. Here's how:

- Look in the blue pages (grey in Manitoba) of your local phone directory under "Government of Canada." Find the "Revenue Canada" section, then "Tax Services" under that. Listed below will be the "TIPS Automated" number—that stands for Tax Information Phone Service.
- Call this number and answer the computer-generated questions. You'll need to have your birth date, social insurance number, and last year's income tax return handy. The TIPS machine will end up telling you what your current RRSP contribution limit is, along with the amount of missed contributions.

4. Now go to your bank, trust, broker, or adviser's office. Open a self-directed RRSP and put all that money in, investing in a mix of government bonds, stocks, and mutual funds that suits your goals, making sure that 20% of it is in foreign content.

And what if you don't have that much extra money? Then borrow it. If you deal with a financial adviser, in many cases he or she has access to capital at even cheaper rates than the banks or trust companies offer. And usually you won't have to start repaying the loan until you get your tax refund, which should be used to pay down part of the loan.

3. CONTRIBUTE AT THE RIGHT TIME

Every year people make the same mistake. They contribute to an RRSP exactly 12 months later than they should have. And, man, do they ever pay for it.

The rules say we all have until 60 days after the end of a taxation year to make a contribution that can be used to reduce taxes in that year. That's why every January and February have been turned into an RRSP orgy as the sellers of retirement funds remind us that this big deadline is looming. Sure, it is a good thing to put money into a plan at any time, but by always making that contribution at the very end of the allowable period, instead of at the beginning, you lose an entire year in which that money could have been growing tax-free.

Don't think it matters much? Putting in $3500 at the beginning of the year, instead of at the end, in a mutual fund earning 10% (and most are doing much better than that) will give you almost $60,000 more after 30 years.

> ***That, of course, is money for nothing: No additional contribution. No borrowing. No pain. No risk. All you have done to earn it is change the day on which you made the contribution.***

This is especially significant since the number of years that you can contribute to an RRSP was reduced a couple of years back. Perhaps, down the line, a further reduction could be on the way (see Chapter 13).

So, contribute to your RRSP early in the year, by all means, but do it a year early. And you can also get on a monthly plan to have RRSP money debited from your paycheque or chequing account on a regular basis.

Did you know . . .

. . . in less than 15 years, according to the *Canadian Medical Association Journal*, 1 million pensioners who are not living in institutions will have some level of disability? Of those, about 10% will require assistance with basic functions—bathing and eating—and another 30% will not be able to manage other chores such as shopping, meal preparation, or housework on their own.

4. MAXIMIZE YOUR CASH FLOW

One chronic complaint I hear from people who miss making their RRSP contributions is that there's no money left at the end of the month to put towards retirement.

Well, we can fix that by using this strategy. Most middle-class people work for paycheques. Federal and provincial income taxes are deducted from those cheques by employers who, by law, have to remit the money on a regular basis.

Most people think there's nothing they can do about this. But they're wrong. You can reduce the tax being withheld and maximize your cash flow. The key is making that RRSP contribution either at the beginning of the taxation year, or in monthly instalments. This way you can increase your cash flow by reducing your paycheque taxes. Instead of waiting a year for that RRSP tax refund cheque, you get it in every pay period.

Here's what to do:

- Make your entire yearly contribution in January (14 months before the actual deadline for that year), borrowing the money if necessary.
- Set up monthly contributions to your plan, using pre-authorized withdrawals from your chequing account, just the way you would with car payments.
- Now, call the local district taxation office of Revenue Canada and ask for the phone number for Source Deductions. These are the folks to whom your employer sends the money that is deducted from your paycheque.
- Call Source Deductions and tell them you want your withholding tax adjusted because you have made or are making RRSP contribution payments. Tell them you want a Tax Deduction Waiver. They'll ask for your estimated income for this year and expected deductions, and you'll have to provide proof of the RRSP contribution.
- Revenue Canada will consider this, then, when approved, send the waiver to your employer, who can reduce the amount of tax taken off your paycheque. This process takes about a month, and you have to do it every year in order to get the tax break.
- Now, your paycheque is going to be fatter. So don't squander it on incidentals. You could take that money and simply increase your mortgage payments, shortening the time before your mortgage is completely paid off (so you can replace it with a tax-deductible investment mortgage).

That extra money would be ideal to purchase mutual fund units on a monthly basis, again through pre-authorized debits that you will never miss. A few years of doing that and you'll be astonished at how much further ahead you are.

The bottom line here is pretty simple: Either you are a serious, long-term, dedicated RRSP contributor, or you are gambling with your future. Amateur investors line up in the snow on the last day of February to put money into an RRSP investment they barely understand.

Pros like you set up a yearly program with a financial adviser and then reap the benefits—more compound income by contributing early, more after-tax income to invest, and a much larger portfolio thanks to a disciplined approach.

It's not as sexy as winning the lottery or being the first to invest in Bre-X (and we all know how that turned out), but it's a heck of a lot more certain.

5. TAKE YOUR SPOUSE TO THE BANK

Even with the federal government investigating the possibility of tax cuts, most Canadians will still pay too much tax. Taxes are wealth killers. That is where an RRSP comes in. It can let you move as many assets as possible into the hands of the least-taxed spouse. In other words, use split income.

Seniors are sitting ducks for increased government taxation—especially well-off seniors who, ironically, were the ones who prepared for retirement. Clawbacks of pension benefits will only increase. The best defence is to even out income flow between you and your spouse. Start doing that now, no matter how far off retirement is.

The best and easiest way to split income is with spousal RRSPs. As outlined in the section on spousal plans in Chapter 5, you can contribute as much as you want, up to your limit (this year's contribution,

Source: Horsey, Seattle Post

plus past unused ones, plus the overcontribution), to your spouse's RRSP. This money becomes your spouse's property, as long as it's left in the plan for three years. And your contributing money to the spousal plan doesn't prevent your spouse from also contributing to a separate personal plan. You don't even need to be married—common-law is okay but, to date, you do have to be of the opposite sex.

Let's say that through spousal RRSPs you were each able to take $28,000 income from retirement plans, instead of one spouse making $56,000. You'd pay 10% less income tax and give up far fewer pension benefits.

Unfortunately many of today's retired Canadians are in the very unhappy position of having virtually all family income flow through the hands of just one spouse. They pay vastly more tax than other couples with equal income split between them. No, it's not fair, and it won't be getting fairer any time soon. But you can avoid the situation.

Spousal RRSPs are one way of doing so. Paying your less-taxed spouse's taxes are another way. Or paying your spouse or children a salary is also permitted, along with bankrolling a spouse's business so that all profits are attributed to him or her, not to you.

6. MAKE THAT OVERCONTRIBUTION

You are allowed to contribute up to $2000 more into your plan than the rules normally allow. Do it now, before this provision becomes history in some future budget. There are several reasons why:

- First, it's hard enough getting enough money into your RRSP, where it grows tax-free, so even though you don't get a tax break for the overcontribution, it's still worth sheltering the money.
- Carrying around an extra $2000 in your RRSP is a good idea. Should you get laid off or lose your job, and don't have enough earned income to make an RRSP contribution next year, you can use that money instead, and you will also get a deduction on your taxes.
- If you have a dependant aged 19 or older, make the overcontribution in his or her name if the child does not have earned income and can't contribute to their own plan. You don't get a tax deduction, but when your child reaches age 59, the $2000 could have turned into $90,000. Demand that they buy you a Porsche.
- Or, if you are retired but still have earned income (like from a rental house), make the overcontribution. As long as you continue to have earned income, you can claim the deduction yearly at the rate of 18% of income, until the $2000 is exhausted. Ditto for a spousal plan.

7. GET A LOAN WITH NO INTEREST

This is a strategy only for first-time home buyers who can withdraw up to $20,000 each ($40,000 for a couple) to use as a down payment on a home—new or resale.

It is, in effect, an interest-free and tax-free loan from your RRSP, which has to be paid back in equal instalments over 15 years. Miss a payment and it becomes taxable as part of your income in that year. You have at least two years before repayment has to start.

But be wary.

Given the long-term decline in residential real estate values, it probably does not make any sense to take money out of your RRSP to buy a home—certainly not while financial markets are showering double-digit rates of return on mutual fund investors.

Critics have always said that the Home Buyers' Plan corrupted the spirit of the RRSP program, and I now agree. But in the true spirit of that corruption, first-time home buyers might as well take advantage of loopholes that were never intended. Here goes:

- If you are a couple in the 40% tax bracket with $20,000 saved for a down payment, along with built-up, missed RRSP contributions, then make those contributions now.
- Then go house-hunting, making sure you do not close a deal prior to 90 days after you made the RRSP contribution.
- Cash in the RRSP, tax-free under the Home Buyers' Plan.
- Add to that the $8000 Ottawa sent you in tax refunds because you contributed to your RRSP (which you then actually spent on a house). Now you have $28,000 to put down, and a smaller mortgage.
- The $20,000 will have to be paid back into your RRSP starting in the year 2002 at the rate of $1300 a year. If you can do it faster, it's to your benefit—get those assets working harder again, and sooner.

As a matter of fact . . .

. . . if you take $5000 out of your RRSP 30 years before retirement, and that amount compounds annually at 10%, you could end up with $85,000 less savings in your golden years. And there's no way you can get that $5000 back in later when you're flush. Be wary of resorting to RRSP withdrawals if you need money—exhaust all other avenues first.

8. NO CASH? NO PROBLEM

So many people miss making an RRSP contribution because they don't have enough cash saved up by the time the annual deadline passes. Silly them!

> ***You don't need money to make an RRSP contribution. All you need are some assets. The government will pay you for selling yourself what you already own.***

The rules are crystal clear. You are allowed to move assets that are currently subject to tax into your tax-free RRSP, to the limit of your annual contribution, and then claim this as a tax deduction just as if you'd contributed saved-up cash.

It's called "contributions in kind," and it's a terrific way for people to catch up on their tax-sheltered retirement savings. It's also a strategy that every investor should employ to reduce the tax load. Remember the example I used earlier of a person with savings bonds but no RRSP—we used this strategy to turn $7000 into $39,000:

- We opened a self-directed RRSP.
- Then we transferred the savings bonds into the plan, and cashed them in.
- Next, we borrowed $2800 from the bank, which was paid off in full two months later with the tax refund cheque we got for transferring the CSBs into the RRSP.
- At that point, we had enough in the RRSP to purchase a Government of Ontario strip bond maturing in 2010, with a maturity value of $39,000. It can be held to maturity or sold off earlier for a capital gain if interest rates drop.

> ***This would be outrageous if it were not perfectly legal. And the shame of it is that most Canadians are completely unaware that this kind of thing can be done simply with just a phone call.***

How many people are out there with no sheltered retirement savings plans, who at the same time have money in GICs, savings bonds, term deposits, savings accounts, and other brain-dead investments that they could be leveraging higher, tax-free?

DO YOU OWN ANY OF THESE?
THEY CAN GO INTO A SELF-DIRECTED PLAN

Canada Savings Bonds	GICs
Provincial Savings Bonds	Mutual fund units
Cash	Labour fund units
Corporate bonds	Limited partnerships
Government of Canada bonds	Stocks
Provincial Government bonds	Mortgages
Term deposits	Small business shares

These assets don't qualify

Foreign currency	Gold, silver
Real estate	Commodities

9. HOLD YOUR OWN MORTGAGE

As outlined in Chapter 8, it is possible to put your own residential mortgage inside your RRSP and make mortgage payments to yourself. Let's review why this is a cool idea. It amounts to a regular, forced transfer of wealth from your income stream into your RRSP. By setting it up properly, you can exceed your annual allowed contribution limits. And you don't end up making the bank richer.

The process is a bit complicated. You will need the help of a competent financial adviser, and it does cost money—about a thousand bucks—to set up, and then several hundred dollars a year to administer.

You also need a lot of cash, or cashable investments, in your RRSP—enough to write a new mortgage that will replace the one you already have in place. And don't forget that wriggling out of a bank mortgage before its term expires can be difficult and costly.

Next, you need a self-directed RRSP. It will lend enough money to discharge the existing mortgage, replace it with a new one, and take title to the property (that means you need a lawyer, too).

Once that is in place, you make regular mortgage payments every month into your RRSP. As I mentioned, Revenue Canada dictates that the mortgage rate must be comparable with existing current rates.

That means you can't issue yourself a 2% home loan. But then, you don't want to do that, because you want to give yourself the highest possible mortgage rate—because the idea is to use this device to squeeze as much of your income as possible into the RRSP. This is not a device for making real estate more affordable. Instead, it's a strategy to bloat your retirement savings.

You also have to insure the mortgage, and you must qualify for it financially, just as if you were going to the bank. Finally, the whole thing has to be administered by an unrelated lender (typically a trust company). And if you don't carefully follow all the rules, Revenue Canada will simply disqualify the deal and your taxes will throb.

The bottom line, however, is that this is very much worth doing as an aggressive RRSP strategy. And it makes even more sense when your RRSP lends out money to finance an income-generating property like a rental house. Then the interest payments you are making into your own RRSP are deductible from your taxable income. Have you heard of double taxation? This is the opposite.

10. PUT YOUR HOUSE TO WORK

In the first half of your life, it makes a lot of sense to acquire and pay off real estate. In the second half, use your real estate as a tool to gain more financial assets or as a source of equity to invest in financial assets. Never forget that the long-term investment trend with an aging population and lots of house-rich and cash-poor baby boomers is from real assets to financial assets. Your RRSP can certainly help.

If you have a paid-up, mortgage-free home, then it represents a lot of money—often hundreds of thousands of dollars—typically earning peanuts (if anything) in capital appreciation. At least a portion of this money could, and should, be out working in the global economy where it can easily be making double-digit returns.

Did you know . . .

. . . it pays off handsomely to remortgage a home? By investing the money into mutual funds, you can create a tax-deductible mortgage. Because the proceeds of the mortgage are used to buy financial assets yielding a greater return than the cost of the mortgage, you get to write off the interest payments from your taxable income. In tax terms, it's not considered to be a mortgage, but an investment loan. But it sure looks and smells like a mortgage to your RRSP.

So, if you have enough cash in your retirement plan (or cashable assets), you can take over that mortgage (subject to the conditions mentioned above) and start enjoying several benefits, namely:

- Liberating your previously locked-in, underperforming equity, so it can go out and multiply.
- Creating a sizeable tax deduction and increasing your after-tax income.
- Giving you a greater ability to shovel money into your RRSP through the vehicle of an RRSP mortgage.

"Most people don't start seriously saving for retirement until age 49. While it would be nice to start saving for retirement when you're 25, unfortunately most people can't do it."

—Graham Byron, Certified Financial Planner, Midland Walwyn Capital Inc.

Chapter 10

Living with Lucien and other Canadian realities

The separation factor
Contribute now—claim later
Diversification
The lowdown on labour funds
Creditors and your RRSP
Going with the flow
Strip bonds appealing
Scaling the maturity ladder
Leaving the Great White North

If you can use any or all of the 10 strategies presented in the previous chapter, you're well on your way to financial security in your retirement years. Here are a few more paths to take, along with a few words of caution that, if heeded, will minimize the bumps along the way.

LUCIEN BOUCHARD–PROOF YOUR WEALTH

The war of words between Ottawa and Quebec City still flares up occasionally, but for the past year or two, things have been rather low key. And it's no wonder: Popular support in that province for a separate

Quebec is nowhere near as high as it once was. There's more than a general dissatisfaction with the PQ government, and it appears that Jean Charest's Liberals could surpass the popularity of Lucien Bouchard and company.

Nevertheless, it is still impossible to know what the ultimate outcome will be—a stronger Canada, a fractured one, or another 20 years of uncertainty. Above all, financial markets hate uncertainty and, for the last 17 years, that's what they've had from Canada.

In any case, let's face the facts: The PQ almost won the October 30, 1995, referendum. Terrified investors dumped millions of dollars in stock and bond funds in the weeks leading up to this referendum.

And the day after the referendum, when financial markets rallied dramatically, all those people who sold decided to buy back again—in keeping with the typical Canadian investment strategy of waiting for a crisis so we can sell low and then buy high! What were they thinking?

The day after the referendum each major bank no-load firm saw about $50 million flow back. At the Bank of Commerce, $47 million coursed into equities and bonds, while at Altamira, president Philip Armstrong noted it was "wall-to-wall buying" as the company handled more than 2000 phone calls.

This, of course, is panic, knee-jerk investing. And it just about guarantees that you will lose money.

There is a way to partially protect yourself from the fray, and that is to make sure you are completely topped up on foreign content in your RRSP (as outlined in Chapters 4 and 5).

Rich people know this. A study done a couple of years back by Environics for the Royal Bank showed that foreign investment and wealth go hand in hand. Among the country's top 10% income earners, 68% own some form of global investments. In sharp contrast, while almost 70% of wealthy people have international investments, just 28% of all Canadians polled by a Royal Trust survey intended to put RRSP money into foreign holdings.

As we've discussed, the rules allow you to have 20% of your total RRSP book value in foreign content. The Canadian dollar has eroded steadily over the last few years, against both the American dollar and other major currencies, like the yen. With the Quebec situation unresolved, with the possibility of another referendum, and with Canada still adding billions to its debt each year, the loonie is always at risk.

Source: Dusan Petricic, Toronto Star

With more national unity problems the currency could easily test its all-time low of about 62 cents U.S. If, in your mind, that is even a remote possibility, why not take action today to ensure that a good chunk of your retirement assets goes up, not down, on the dollar's decline?

Now is the time to be prudent: Review your portfolio with a financial adviser. If you like fixed-income investments, then buy a Government of British Columbia or Ontario bond that pays in yen. If you want to buy shares in the Royal Bank, go for preferred shares that give dividends in U.S. dollars. Seek out and invest in Canadian companies that earn most of their income offshore. Actions like these will help preserve your wealth when separation talk comes up again.

DO IT NOW, ENJOY IT LATER

This strategy allows people who know they will be making more money later to maximize their tax savings. If you know your earnings will rise, then make the RRSP contribution today (so the money can compound free of tax), but save the official tax receipt for later. There is nothing in the rules that says the receipt has to be attached to the annual tax return for the year in which the contribution was made.

This strategy will work for a salesperson in a cyclical industry (like real estate) who wants to keep making RRSP contributions, but saves up the receipts to offset income earned in a good year. It will work for a graduating professional just starting to build a practice, or for a high-salaried woman on maternity leave.

In these instances the tax receipt will actually be worth more in tax savings later—so why not hang on to it? Just keep good records and don't lose the receipts. Getting a financial institution to re-issue lost receipts is possible, but growing an oak tree is usually faster.

Did you know . . .

. . . that over the past 20 years the average age of retirement has dropped from 65 to nearly 60? The sharp drop between 1986 and 1987 was a result of the minimum age for CPP benefits being dropped from 65 to 60. In the nineties, the retirement age has continued to slide, largely due to downsizing, corporate buyouts for older staff, etc. Combined with the expanding life expectancies and the continued trend to early retirement, you can understand how important it is to assemble a solid nest egg to support a retirement that can often be as long as your working life.

MIX IT UP

And I don't mean donning gloves and going after the person who advised you, late in the game, to put everything you have into Bre-X. As the old proverb cautions, "Don't put all your eggs into one basket." Wise investors know that. Diversification is the great equalizer when it comes to ups and downs in the marketplace. However, failing to adequately mix up your portfolio is not the biggest stumble you can make.

The single greatest mistake Canadian investors make is trying to do their own financial planning. The second mistake flows out of the first because most of us are wimps—and we attempt to avoid all risk when it comes to investing. We happily travel the highways of this country

Source: The Globe and Mail

dodging flying truck wheels and Indy circuit wannabes, but when it comes to our money, we're overcautious to a fault. That's why most RRSPs end up in the bank invested in GICs.

The worst investment you can make is a GIC. Interest rates are low, and staying low while inflation is slight, maybe even heading to borderline deflation. The combination is deadly, especially for baby boomers who need to earn double-digit returns for the next 15 years.

GIC investors usually have no idea they can earn a much higher rate of return, while taking less risk, with a government strip bond. Even more importantly, most Canadians have no idea that few investments are safer over the long haul than the stock market. The long-term direction of stocks is up. Yes, there are periods of volatility after stock values rise too quickly, but those should be viewed as buying opportunities.

Most Canadians have no idea that the market is so safe. They do not realize that stock values reflect technological advances, medical breakthroughs, and economic expansion. If you have any faith in the future—and I have all kinds of it—then equities are the place to be. Just remember to buy quality stocks and mutual funds.

But beware of "hot" stocks—the ones that get headline attention because they soar in value, making early investors rich. About the worst thing that has happened lately was the meteoric rise and spectacular free fall of Bre-X Minerals Ltd. But Bre-X investors weren't the only ones who took a beating. The initial success of early Bre-X investors had countless others running around looking for the next junior mining stock miracle. But the odds were against them. And a lot of people lost a lot of money.

This is not investing. It's a crapshoot. Remember these rules:

- Hot stocks get cold really fast. By the time the newspapers notice a flaming stock, it has already peaked. If you want to play the stock market, make sure you keep an eye on what the stock promoters and insiders are doing with their holdings. When they start to bail, go with them. And never, ever, put all your financial resources into that one play—5% or 10% of your portfolio's worth will give you a good return if the stock soars. If it doesn't, you won't suffer an irreversible setback.
- It is always better to diversify. Don't invest in only one stock; invest in 10. Don't invest in just one sector of the economy, but in several. More diversity equals less risk.
- The best, easiest diversification comes from using mutual funds. You buy less risk along with superior management. Be careful not to diversify too much, or you can water down your returns. A maximum of eight or nine funds will get the job done, and seems to be the top limit suggested by many experts.
- Buy shares in companies with proven track records. Your financial adviser can get you reams of information on a stock's history. The Internet is also an excellent source of performance data.
- Increase your holdings when stock values fall. Corrections are inevitable and, as I write this—with North American stock values at near-record levels—the mother of all corrections could well be around the corner. A dip of 15% would bring the TSE 300 down by more than a thousand points—terrifying many novice market players but posing a huge buying opportunity for long-term investors.

As a matter of fact . . .

. . . don't forget what history proves to us—there is no risk in the stock market for long-term investors. The market will continue to rise as long as humankind continues to advance. So far, I can't find any evidence that a decline has begun.

Conventional investment logic dictates that the first things to go in your RRSP are the ones most heavily taxed when not tax-sheltered. That includes interest-bearing investments like bonds. Other investments, like stocks that pay you dividends or capital gains, should be held outside your RRSP. That way you don't lose the benefit of the dividend tax credit or the more favourable treatment of capital gains.

If you have substantial assets, that rule holds true. But most people don't have the wealth to justify two separate investment portfolios, so they should concentrate on building their RRSP, and making sure that its holdings are diversified.

Always be aware that the greatest risk you face is not losing your money, but rather outliving it. Being content with a low-yielding GIC is false security.

Even beyond the age of 65, investors need to have a strong growth component in their retirement savings, because the odds of living another 25 years are getting better every day. Over that period of time, nothing will perform better than equity-based mutual funds.

THE PAIN OF LABOUR FUNDS

Four years ago it looked like it was impossible to lose by making an RRSP investment in a labour-sponsored venture capital fund. After all, the tax incentives were almost unbelievable: Investors in the top tax bracket got their 50% tax rebate, plus another 40% in federal and provincial tax credits. For an investment of about $500, you could salt away a $5000 asset in your retirement plan.

The labour funds were given this amazingly favourable treatment in order to encourage the growth of pools of capital that would flow into the economy, into small and medium-sized enterprises, creating jobs. It was a nice theory.

And as a result of the tax break, during the 1996 RRSP season investors gorged on these things, pumping millions into them until the total pot stood at about $2 billion. However, like a lot of theories, once they're off the drawing board for a while, it becomes evident they are exactly that—simply, nice theories.

Many funds have not been able to find companies to invest in. Others have nonexistent or poor track records. Too many investors asked too few questions, caring only about the tax savings. As a result, they ended up with bad investments. Meanwhile, critics sniped at the federal and provincial governments for using the tax system to distort peoples' investment decisions. In hindsight, the critics may have been right.

Consider the biggest labour fund, Working Ventures. It had expected to raise $150 million during the 1996 RRSP season. Instead, it raised $350 million. And four months later, President Ron Begg had to tell a roomful of reporters that because the fund had swollen to more than $850 million—while only $170 million had actually been invested in businesses—new unit sales were being cut off for a year. Meanwhile, the fund paid out millions of dollars in penalties because it did not do what it was supposed to—invest more in the economy.

Are labour funds a good investment? Not as good as they used to be. The main reason is that shortly after the 1996 RRSP season, all of the rules changed. The main changes came last year when Finance Minister Paul Martin announced that:

- The federal tax credit was being reduced from 20% to 15%.
- The maximum share purchase eligible for the tax credit was being reduced from $5000 to $3500.
- The minimum holding period for labour fund shares was being increased from five to eight years, including for seniors and retirees. In Quebec, investors must hold the money in a fund until retirement, although it allows people nearing 65, those disabled or unemployed, and those leaving the country to withdraw their money after two years.
- The ability to double-dip has ended. Investors can no longer redeem shares at the end of the holding period and then immediately reinvest the money to get a new set of tax credits. Now, an investor has to wait two years past the year of redemption before being able to invest again and get a tax break.

Other jurisdictions, like Ontario, have followed suit with budget measures that strip away the funds' tax incentives. So now investors who bought units have to decide what course of action to take when they are eligible to sell those units. When redemption time comes around, the current thinking is that investors will toss everything into the lifeboats—including the less-than-modest returns—and bail.

Despite the tax credits, many people feel that they would have been better off investing in regular mutual funds, given the poor performance of most of these funds. In most cases, I'd recommend selling.

As for the rest of them, bail out when you can.

SHIELD YOUR WEALTH FROM CREDITORS

Most people are shocked to learn that RRSP assets are not protected from creditors by federal law. In fact, your investment can be at risk in several ways:

- If your marriage breaks down, provincial law will allow your ex-spouse to make a claim against your RRSP assets. In general, you will lose half.
- If the financial institution holding your RRSP goes belly-up, like Confederation Life did, you lose all assets beyond the insured limit of $60,000 for cash, GIC, term deposits, and so on.
- If you die owing Revenue Canada money for unpaid taxes, your RRSP can be opened under the Income Tax Act, allowing the feds to get their money.
- If you go bankrupt, creditors could get a court order against your RRSP if the money you contributed to it over the last few years could have been used to pay off your bills.

These are some of the threats you face, and there are always new attempts to crack into the pool of RRSP capital. It is a sorry reality that no federal law gives a consistent level of protection from creditors to RRSP investors. Various provincial governments have tried to offer protection—for example, British Columbia provincial law excludes RRSPs from an estate if the plan holder had designated a beneficiary.

And this is exactly what you should do, wherever you live. Name your spouse as the beneficiary on your retirement plan for several reasons—to increase protection from creditors, to allow transfer of the RRSP assets upon death to your spouse, and to avoid probate fees.

Finally, if you think you'll have problems with creditors in the future—or if you just want to be as safe as possible—use a spousal RRSP to harbour your assets (as long as your spouse isn't on the lam from the law). Assets put into a spousal plan become the possessions of your spouse. RRSPs with life insurance companies are also protected from creditors.

Losing anything over the $60,000 liability limit for cash, GICs, and term deposits with a financial institution that fails, makes a strong point for adjusting your portfolio make-up. One way to protect yourself is to convert some or all of these interest-bearing investments into quality mutual funds. Mutual funds are not owned by the financial institution or investment house, but held in trust on your behalf by a bank or trust company.

DON'T FOLLOW THE HERD

The most important thing you can do when investing your RRSP money is to make sure you maintain a long-term view. Most people don't. They assume that today's reality will dictate future situations. But history shows otherwise. Consider the results of two *Business Week* polls done seven years apart:

If you had to choose the one investment that you think would be the best right now, which would it be?

	1980s	1990s
Real Estate	40%	25%
Mutual Funds	8%	24%
Common Stock	5%	10%

The shift away from real assets, including real estate, will only continue as the North American population ages. Billions of dollars will flow into equities and funds for more than a decade, pushing their valuations higher. More and more people will wake up to the fact the single best strategy is for them to drain out the equity in their homes while financial institutions are still offering home equity loans.

In the future, selling a suburban house could be simply impossible. The trend is already taking hold in the United States, where home ownership levels for young people—under 34—are plunging.

As American University professor Peter Chinloy has said, "My guess is that younger people have seen the relatively low appreciation levels for real estate, and are holding more of their assets in stocks and bonds." U.S. National Association of Realtors chief economist John Tucillo says that when the big price drop comes, there's little doubt what kind of housing will be hardest hit: "Undistinguished, middle-class suburban properties."

So, now is the time for middle-aged investors to cash out real estate, or at least to use its equity to acquire financial assets.

Did you know . . .
. . . it took the Dow 44 years to hit the 1000-point mark? It took just 25 more years to crack 8000, and only 189 trading days for the Dow to vault from 8000 to 9000 points.

But will those financial assets—stocks, bonds, and mutual funds—tank in the future the way that real estate is now? Anything is possible, but it's unlikely unless, in the decades to come, there's a bout of hyperinflation triggered by a debt crisis or a major international armed conflict. In circumstances like those, people with their wealth in oil and gold would win. In any case, unwavering demographics would still dictate tough times for real estate, which dances to only one beat: supply and demand.

Right now, the superior investment strategy is a dramatic move into financial assets, with a 10% inflation hedge against calamity through vehicles like an oil and gas fund and a steady reduction in real estate equity.

WHY BUY A GIC WHEN THERE ARE STRIP BONDS?

Any Canadian with any of his or her RRSP assets in a GIC is making a big mistake—interest rates are low, and will stay low. Your investment is locked up for years. There's no potential for a capital gain.

Why would anyone put money in a GIC? There's only one possible answer: People think they're safe. Well, there is an even safer place for retirement money that offers huge advantages over a GIC: strip bonds.

- Strip bonds pay more interest.
- They are cashable at any time.
- They are free of risk. There is no limit similar to the $60,000 insurance threshold for GICs.
- They go up in value when interest rates go down, giving a capital gain.
- They can be purchased at a deep discount to face value.
- And, when safely tucked into your self-directed RRSP, they are virtual money machines—doubling or tripling your investment in a defined period of time.

Why doesn't everyone have strip bonds? Because they don't sell them at most banks, so all of those people trading growth for risk-free GICs are simply not being made aware of the strip-bond alternative.

> ***I think every RRSP ought to contain some government bonds. And let's not confuse strip bonds with Canada Savings Bonds or provincial copycats like Ontario Savings Bonds. Those are tepid little investments scarcely better than GICs, bought by people who actually think they are investing.***

No, real government bonds are different, but as accessible as one phone call to your independent financial adviser. And, like GICs and CSBs, strip bonds are categorized as being "fixed income," because they pay a predetermined amount of interest when held to maturity. But unlike GICs and CSBs, strip bonds fluctuate in value daily, rising or falling in reverse to interest rates, and they can be bought or sold at any time, no matter what maturity date they carry.

"I've reviewed your entire portfolio, Mr. Hartwelder, and I find that your lottery ticket for Saturday's draw is your best shot at financial independence."

Source: David Brown, Toronto Star

SO, WHAT IS A GOVERNMENT STRIP BOND?

Basically, a strip bond is a regular government bond issued by any Canadian province, or other bodies like Ontario Hydro or the Export Development Corporation, as part of the ongoing process of financing government spending. Regular bonds pay investors interest, usually twice a year (although some pay monthly), so they are good for people looking for a steady, guaranteed income.

But brokers can take the bonds and separate them in two—the interest coupons and the principal. As an investor, you can buy either the coupons, which will give you income on a regular basis but no payout at the end, or the bond itself (which is stripped of interest, giving rise to the term "strip" bond), which will pay you face value on the day of maturity or the market value on whatever day prior to maturity that you decide to sell it.

Strip bonds are also issued by corporations, but these are not as secure as government strip bonds because they're backed by corporate assets, rather than the power of taxation. The federal government stopped issuing new bonds in early 1997—good news for taxpayers, but unsettling to the bond market. Corporate bonds are selling like hot-cakes as a result, and there is more downward pressure on interest rates.

That power to tax is exactly what gives strip bonds their security. It's as close to a complete guarantee as you are ever going to get with an investment. During my financial seminars someone will often ask, "But what if the government is broke and defaults on its bonds in future years?" Sure, that could happen. And in that case, the strip bond investor would lose. But . . .

> ***If a Canadian government ever defaulted on a bond issue, that would pretty well be the end of the Canadian dollar—including the ones in your GIC. In such a circumstance you could pretty well forget about the Canada Deposit Insurance Corporation refunding your money. It would be swept away in an instant.***

Because the strip bond pays no interest, you buy it at a big discount to its face value. That means you can leverage a big payout years later with a much smaller amount of money now. The longer the period until the bond matures, the bigger the discount. And the higher the yield on the bond, the cheaper it is to buy.

Did you know . . .

. . . that without a self-directed RRSP, you cannot invest in government bonds, strip bonds, or mortgages?

Here's an example: In May 1994, I bought a Government of Ontario strip bond that matures on February 18, 2002. The annual yield was good at the time—8.86%—and on maturity that bond will be worth $194,000 inside my RRSP. But the actual cost to buy it was $100,412, which worked out to be $51.75 for every $100 worth of bond. In effect, I was arranging to double my money in less than eight years—without any risk.

By investing $100,412 I will receive $93,588 more than I paid in 7.7 years. Where else can you get a yield like that, guaranteed by the government? Not with a GIC.

Now, some people will tell you that these strip bonds are volatile and risky because the market price fluctuates as interest rates rise and fall. But remember this: When interest rates rise, you only lose money if you sell the bond! Hang on to it until maturity and you get exactly what you always knew you'd get: face value.

Regardless of what rates do between now and 2002, I know exactly what my Ontario strip bond will pay into my RRSP, and that's $194,000.

I don't think interest rates are going to rise much, if at all. Rather, I believe that rates are in a long-term decline, along with inflation. That means the odds are that your strip bonds will rise in market value in the future, not fall.

In fact, a year after I bought that Ontario bond for $51.75 per $100, it was selling for $56.38, so I could have unloaded the bond for $109,394 and taken a $9000 capital gain for holding the investment for a year. Because interest rates had fallen, and the bond was a year closer to maturity, it had become more valuable.

Inside my RRSP, that would be realized free of tax, equal to a one-year, 9% return, several points higher than a GIC. Outside my RRSP, the money would be subject to capital gains tax of 36%, substantially less than the tax on GIC interest of 54%.

Government bonds come in maturities ranging from 6 months to 30 years. Shorter-term mini-bonds are called Treasury bills (T-bills), also backed by the power to tax and available in terms of 30, 60, 90, or 180 days.

Some investment firms will "package" together a number of bonds of various types and maturities specifically for RRSPs. Many of these offerings are excellent, and just having access to them alone is worth the effort in finding a good, independent financial adviser.

You can also buy bonds at the bank. But, the bank is not in the business of giving detailed financial advice, so there are still advantages to doing your bond-buying through your personal adviser.

Now, strip bonds are wonderful RRSP instruments, and every portfolio should have some. But make sure that your asset mix is right—and that bonds (fixed income) are held alongside equities and mutual funds.

Outside an RRSP, strips are less attractive, as Revenue Canada will tax you on interest income not yet received. That's the same negative tax situation as a GIC or CSB—so all of these investment vehicles should properly be tax-sheltered.

STRIPS VERSUS GICs: NO CONTEST

Strip bonds	**GICs**
Yield 7% to 8%	Yield 6% (1997 rates)
1 to 30 years	5 years
Cashable anytime	Locked in
Rise when rates fall (capital gain potential)	No fluctuation
Unlimited government guarantee	$60,000 deposit-insurance limit
Buy at discount to face value	Interest paid on maturity
Taxable yearly (except if in RRSP)	Taxable yearly (except if in RRSP)

THE DIFFERENCE BETWEEN MEN AND BONDS

Bonds mature.

And here's a risk-free, long-term investment and retirement strategy you just can't beat. Because strip bonds are purchased at a discount to face value, the longer until a bond matures, the cheaper it is to buy.

Here's an example: When my mother was 81 (I am forbidden from revealing her current age) she decided that she wanted to leave some money in her estate for educating a grandchild—money that wouldn't be needed for 15 years. She could have set aside $8000 from her estate or, better yet, she could spend the money sending herself on a cruise and use just a portion of it to buy a strip bond that would accomplish the same purpose.

So she did. She bought a strip bond maturing in 2010 that would be worth $8000. For each $100 of the bond, she paid just $24.88, so the total cost of buying the bond was $1999. And the interest that will end up in the hands of the grandchild is $6000, plus the bond purchase price.

Every baby boomer should be assembling a ladder of strip bonds with staggered maturity dates to ensure a cash stream in the future. As each strip bond matures, the money can be spent on more strip bonds to keep the ladder going. Once in place, the effect of compounding interest is awesome.

Did you know . . .

. . . that, according to Statistics Canada, almost half of all retired Canadians are living on less that $15,000 annual personal income? The maximum benefits provided by OAS and CPP are around $4847 and $8937, respectively. Don't count on that going up in the future.

Imagine if you expanded on what my mother did. If, for the next 15 years, you put your annual RRSP contribution into a strip bond with a 15-year maturity, then every year, starting in 2015 and lasting until 2030, you'd have money coming due as retirement income.

How much? That depends on the future direction of interest rates. But if we used my mother's example—paying $24.88 for every $100 in maturity value—a $10,000 RRSP contribution made today will ensure a return of $40,192 in 15 years. Yes, that's guaranteed.

Or you can purchase a number of strip bonds with varying maturity dates, with money you may have now inside your RRSP, to get a maturity ladder in place right away.

So, baby boomers now in their forties and fifties can plan for stable retirement income by purchasing strip bonds that mature in 15, 20, or even 30 years. That will mean receiving between $4 and $6 in the future for every $1 invested now. Using a maturity ladder you can leverage each year's allowable RRSP contribution into one more year of financial security decades from now.

WHEN YOU GOTTA GO . . .

Let's face it, we live in a country envied by many the world over. Studies conducted by the United Nations consistently cite Canada at the top of list when it comes to a place on this overcrowded planet in which one can live peacefully, productively, and prosperously. So who would want to leave? Well, at times, you have to.

Whether it's pursuing a career abroad for a few years or snapping the old snow shovel in half and retiring to a warmer clime, you should discuss any move with your financial adviser to ensure that there are no unpleasant taxation consequences.

For example, if you are retiring to the United States, do not withdraw a lump sum from your RRSP before heading south. This will trigger a big tax bite (up to 50% in the highest marginal tax bracket). It's best to wait to withdraw funds until you've given up your Canadian residency. Once you are a resident of the U.S. or any other country you've taken a liking to, the most that Revenue Canada will demand is a 25% withholding tax on any withdrawals. That rate drops to 15% on periodic withdrawals as opposed to lump sum withdrawals.

On taking up residency status down south, you can also take steps to ensure that you minimize tax paid to the IRS. Those steps involve increasing the cost base of your assets, in other words, your book value. This can be done without adding any more money to your RRSP, and should be undertaken before assuming U.S. residency. If your current assets' market value is, say, $500,000, and this has grown from your book value of $100,000 (the original purchase price of the assets), just sell your assets and reinvest the $500,000 (even in the same investments).

Why would you do this? Well, now that your book value is $500,000, you can withdraw that entire amount without paying tax in the U.S. Because this strategy of upping the cost base is conducted inside your RRSP, you will not face a tax bill from Ottawa. However, you will probably face some costs in terms of commissions. Be aware that transferring your assets from one RRSP institution to another does not increase the book value.

Also, the U.S. Securities and Exchange Commission (SEC) has begun to crack down on individuals managing their RRSPs—American law frowns on resident investors buying or trading securities that are not registered in the U.S. As a Canadian investor living Stateside, you can continue to hold your funds without making changes, or you can redeem them. You could also provide a trusted individual with the power of attorney to make decisions on your behalf north of the border.

Another option is to dump your money into an asset allocation program before heading to the U.S. That way you're not required to make any decisions. You could also make the odd trip back to the frigid north to conduct your business, but that could end up upsetting the folks at the SEC.

There are all sorts of tax rules and regulations involved in moving out of the country. Again, a thorough discussion with your accountant and financial adviser can ensure that you maximize advantageous strategies when taking off.

HIGHLY RECOMMENDED:

- Maximize your RRSP foreign content limit to offset the fluctuating loonie.
- Make your annual contribution, but save the receipt for next year if you believe you'll be earning more then.
- Diversify your portfolio, but stay away from so-called "hot-stocks."
- Be very cautious about investing in labour-sponsored funds; get some advice before you do so.
- Make sure you've done all that's possible to protect your RRSP assets from creditors.
- Don't follow the traditional approach to investing; adapt to today's new reality—financial assets.
- Forget GICs and take a look at the flexibility, solid returns, and minimal risk of strip bonds.
- When leaving Canada to reside in another country, get professional advice to avoid big tax headaches.

"To maintain the same standard of living all your life, you will have to maximize your RRSPs. Does it happen a lot? No. Should people be a little worried? Yes."
—Clay Gillespie, Financial Adviser, Rogers Group Financial Ltd.

Chapter 11

Preparation for every generation!

Generation X
Baby boomers
Junior seniors
Senior seniors

Far too many Canadians believe there is a one-kind-fits-all investment strategy for successful retirement planning. Usually it goes like this: Get married, buy a house, pay it off, invest in risk-free RRSP assets like bonds and GICs, sell the house for big bucks, move into a condo and spend six months of the year being irradiated in Arizona or Florida. Ah, if life only were that simple.

Unfortunately, there are some giant flaws in that plan. Real assets like real estate have a limited future. The return on "safe" and traditional retirement assets, like bonds and GICs, is much too low to keep pace with increased longevity. North America is trying to digest the world's biggest demographic bulge, which will distort financial markets for the next two decades. And, just to make you really nervous, be aware that your marriage has a 50-50 chance of dissolving, which means that family retirement assets may be carved in half.

On top of that, the Canada Pension Plan is in deep trouble—no matter what tinkering is done to it—which means that baby boomers may never see a government cheque in old age.

And then there are the Generation Xers, likely destined to pay more in taxes for a less certain future than the self-absorbed, live-for-today boomers who went before them, and who were largely responsible for some $600 billion in public debt.

Getting concerned, anguished, and depressed about the picture painted here? I don't blame you. But, I still believe that despite all of these obstacles, the future—the next decade and a half—will be wonderful for those who adopt the right investment strategies. No matter what age demographic you belong to.

Financial markets will sparkle, while the cost of living will stay low. Technology will continue to create unheard-of new opportunities, interest rates will stay on a low plateau, and your assets could double every 60 months without taking on more risk than, say, driving through Winnipeg.

But you've got to know what to do, and when to do it. Now, more than ever, investment strategies must be appropriate to your age. Here are my basic suggestions:

TWENTYSOMETHINGS

You have not been dealt a fair hand, but make the most of it. The baby boomers will live longer than any generation before them, hanging on to their jobs as long as possible and costing a fortune in retirement benefits. Even if public pensions will not be there for them (a highly likely scenario), their health care bill alone will be staggering.

That spells even higher taxes and, worse, a declining economy starting sometime after 2015. Things will get ugly for the same reason they are now streaking higher—demographics. The current North American economy will be robust for years to come. But after that, with millions of 60-year-olds around, economic growth could flame out fast.

Here's what you must do:

You cannot afford to waste time—You have to invest aggressively now, and for the next 15 years.

Maximize your RRSPs—Catch up on missed contributions even if you have to borrow the money to do so—it makes sense with today's low loan rates and the corresponding tax refund. Make the $2000 over-contribution. Income-split with your spouse as a long-term hedge against job loss.

Invest RRSP assets in high-growth investments—Equities and equity-based mutual funds are the only place to be. When the market corrects itself, step up your investment pace. The Dow and the TSE 300 are going higher over the next few years—this is your best chance to build significant wealth quickly.

Be aggressive—Recognize obvious opportunities. The Internet is revolutionizing communications, and has only just begun to have an impact on consumers. Technology stocks will explode further in value and an aging population will require far more health care than the public system can deliver. Wise investors will put money into nursing and retirement home companies, medical care providers, biotech firms, and health care venture capitalists.

Adopt a sensible real estate strategy—Now is an excellent time to be a first-time home buyer—so, go ahead, buy. That will stabilize your housing costs and allow you to build up other financial assets more quickly. Later on it will provide some equity on which to draw. But be careful. The real estate market could collapse within 15 years. Don't get caught. Buy a house you can see yourself living in for a long time.

BABY BOOMERS

What's to become of them? They're a big generation with big problems. But they also have huge chances to accumulate serious wealth. Boomers are in terrible shape, having saved just about 5% of what will be needed to finance their retirements.

Too few boomers appreciate what is happening. Within 35 years—when the average baby boomer will be 75—the number of retired people will have surged by 142%, while the entire Canadian population will have grown by just 15%. By 2015 half the population will be over 40 for the first time in history.

While many Canadians still continue their love affair with GICs, long-term investors seeking better returns are looking elsewhere. This has prompted many financial institutions to offer juiced-up versions of the traditional GIC, and initiate more aggressive and appealing marketing programs.

Did you know . . .

. . . that, according to Statistics Canada, most Canadians can be expected to live for almost another 20 years beyond 65? And only half of that time will they be free of any disability.

Imagine the pressures that will be put on the economy. And on health care. As Barbara Beck of *The Economist* has pointed out, "90%

of the cost of medical care people consume over their lifetime is incurred in the six months before their death." If this is depressing you, it should. That's the point.

Demographics are no longer on our side. Boomers will overwhelm the public pension system and bankrupt public health care. If you want a happy, prosperous retirement, then you will have to earn it. Do not expect a single dollar in government pensions. And expect to pay a substantial amount for adequate medical care.

Do not assume that the services today's seniors receive—pension cheques and income supplements, free medical care and drugs, and cheap nursing home rates—will be there for retired boomers. Expect to be on your own financially.

> ***This reality dictates an aggressive investment and tax strategy for the next 15 or 20 years. You still have time. You can do it even if you are 45 and have saved nothing so far. Using RRSP actions I have outlined, there is no reason to fear what's coming. You can be ready. Here's how:***

- ***You cannot afford to miss a single RRSP contribution.***
- ***You must reduce your tax profile by every means possible.***
- ***You must achieve double-digit rates of return on your investments.***
- ***You cannot afford to invest in a GIC or savings bond.***
- ***You have to raise your tolerance for risk.***
- ***You must reconsider your real estate assets.***

Fortunately for all baby boomers, salvation is at hand. You can dodge the demographic bullet, due to the incredible convergence of low inflation, falling interest rates, and rising financial markets. This is a historic opportunity to grow your wealth. The great second chance. Here's how to start:

You can no longer be savers—You have to be investors. The returns that boomers need simply will not be found in interest-bearing assets. You have to invest more aggressively in stock and bond markets and in mutual funds, especially in equity funds. Sure, there is

'Yes, Mrs. Hartwelder, we do have an alternative to fixed-income securities. . .'

Source: David Brown, Toronto Star

more risk and volatility involved, but buy and hold quality investments, ride out fluctuations, and a decade from now I am certain you will have increased your wealth in a way not possible with GICs, CSBs, etc.

Catch up on missed RRSP contributions—This includes the $2000 overcontribution. Borrow to do this if you have to.

Use self-directed RRSPs—Give yourself maximum investment flexibility. Don't be talked into a GIC-type RRSP. Do not be deterred by the non-tax-deductible fee—this is money well spent.

Invest for growth—Boomers need to be at least 75% invested in stocks or equity-based mutual funds. The less you have accumulated so far, the more aggressive the funds should be. You need double-digit rates of return to grow the average baby boomer RRSP of $30,000 into at least $500,000 a decade and a half from now.

Did you know . . .

. . . that the baby boomers' quest for stocks and mutual funds could power the TSE 300 to 20,000 points within the next decade? So says David Cork, author of *The Pig and the Python*. He believes that the shortage of stocks in Canada—compounded by the 20% foreign content rule—could create days that are opposite to the 1987 correction. The market could soar on a buying panic because there's an absence of sellers. Your best bet? Buy now and see your fund values tower skyward later.

Find better alternatives to your GICs—If you can't sleep at night with all your money in volatile funds, and feel that fixed-income assets are more your style, you can acquire assets with a better return than GICs. Wait until your GICs mature, cash them in, and invest in government strip bonds. You will get a greater rate of return, the potential for a capital gain if interest rates fall further, and more security because there's no limit to the amount the government will guarantee. They're also fully cashable at any time.

Cash out real estate equity—For many boomers this will be the hardest step emotionally, because we matured in an era when real estate equalled wealth. But those days are over. The trend now is away from real assets and towards financial assets. In the future it will be harder to sell your home—the real estate market will never in your lifetime come back to the pace of the 1980 boom. The best thing you can do is unlock the equity in your home—now likely earning a zero rate of return—and get it into growth funds. You can do this by selling your home and downsizing to the kind of real estate that does have a future, or by taking out a home equity loan and creating a tax deduction at the same time.

Get professional financial help—The greatest mistake most people make is thinking they can figure all of this out for themselves. Most can't. Most fail. Most believe that relying on the expertise of a financial adviser will cost them a lot of money or that they'll be soaked for commissions. Those are dangerous myths.

I would not dream of managing my own portfolio. I also wouldn't try to fix the hard drive on my computer or the timing belt on my car, so why would I try to pick the best nine mutual funds out of about 2000? Experts are experts for a very good reason—they know this stuff.

Hedge against the loonie—That's right—*je me souviens*. The premier of Quebec is a separatist and he says there will be another referendum on sovereignty. Financial markets hate uncertainty and the dollar is at risk as long as the threat of a referendum is in the air. It is simply not prudent to have all your wealth in Canadian dollars. That means investing in international mutual funds, foreign-denominated bonds, foreign currency dividend income, and a lot of other, Bouchard-proof investments. I'll bet even he's got some.

JUNIOR SENIORS

Lots of people aged 55 to 75 make the same mistake, thinking they cannot afford to take any risk with their investments and must be satisfied with nothing more than pension and interest income. Wrong. In fact, dangerous. First, you will pay the most tax on pension and interest payments.

Second, people in their sixties often fail to budget for the future. But they should. After all, they stand a very good chance of living another 20 years or more and have a huge risk of running out of money before they pass on. Also, the last years of life can often be the most costly, requiring expensive medical care or special housing.

Third, interest rates have declined substantially, so fixed-income investments like GICs will only offer less income in the future, not more. It's time to cash them in and find something better. Here's how:

Replace maturing GICs with bonds—Investments like mortgage-backed securities are a fine idea. You will earn a greater return with less risk and more flexibility and potential for a capital gain. When your GICs mature, view it as an opportunity to get some of that capital invested for far greater returns, because . . .

You should be 50% invested for growth—That means quality stocks and quality equity-based mutual funds. Break the interest-only mentality that keeps seniors' incomes far lower than they need to be.

Use a systematic withdrawal plan for income—This is a great way of taking money out of a mutual fund on a regular basis, and you will pay substantially less tax than you would getting an income stream from a GIC or a pension. Why? Because the fund pays you capital gains, which are taxed at a far lower rate. And their long-term performance is far superior to any return you can get on fixed-income investments.

A $100,000 investment in Trimark's Canadian-dollar fund in 1981 would have given you a $10,000 annual income and be worth about $500,000 today. Or $100,000 invested in Fidelity Growth America in 1990 would have paid the same and today be worth more than $300,000. You'd have money at your disposal and your capital would keep amassing. All of the quality mutual fund firms offer withdrawal plans that your financial adviser can tailor to meet your long-term income needs.

As a matter of fact . . .

. . . using a systematic withdrawal plan comes in really handy when leveraging the equity in your home. If you take out an interest-only loan of $50,000, $100,000, or more against your home and then put the money into a quality mutual fund, you can have the fund make monthly payments to the bank to cover the loan. Not only will the fund continue to deliver a solid return, but the money it pays to take care of the loan can be deducted from your income tax. You win on two counts. Your assets grow and your taxes go down.

Don't sit on real estate equity—Why have tens of thousands of dollars in real estate, earning you nothing, when that money could be yielding income—financing travel, building an estate for your children, or simply giving you a superior quality of life? At your age, real estate can turn into a trap—expensive to maintain and insure. If you are over the age of 50, you should seriously question how much of your wealth you can afford to keep in a non-performing asset like your home.

Get moving on sensible estate planning—If you do not plan properly, your estate will be decimated by taxes, and your wishes may not be carried out. If you die owning real estate, it may saddle your children with a huge tax liability. How about probate fees and power of attorney? Have you named beneficiaries for your RRSPs? Have you estimated what your terminal tax return might look like? Do you have a will and an executor? If you answered no to any of these questions, don't hesitate to take action. Dying is a complicated process. You've got to be ready or it could mean real financial hardship for those you leave behind.

SENIOR SENIORS

Yes, things finally start to get simpler when you are 75 or older. But with longevity on the rise, people in this age bracket still have a lot of living to do. As mentioned already, these years can be some of the most expensive, especially for those who are in slowly declining health. Bear these points in mind:

Dump the GICs—There is simply no reason to be locking up money for long, five-year periods just to get a return of far less than 10%. The yield will be far higher from a government bond (not a savings bond) and you will still have liquidity—the ability to cash it in at any time if your circumstances change.

Maintain a growth component in your portfolio—You should still have at least 25% of your assets invested in equity-based mutual funds or quality stocks to give you dividend income. The growth will help finance the next decade and tax implications are far more favourable. As with junior seniors, you should be using a systematic withdrawal plan to get regular income from these mutual funds.

Sell real estate now—There is no solid financial reason not to. The capital could be earning a lot more in the economy than in your house. The current real estate market is more buoyant than it's been in some time, and you might get a better price today than in a year or two. A house is costly to keep, and a lot of quality retirement housing is coming onstream in virtually every major Canadian centre. It's time to move.

Get a financial adviser you trust—You need an effective estate plan, along with proper tax planning and investment strategies. If you have not worked with an adviser in the past, this is a good time to start.

Go for a cruise—That is what it's all about—the financial security to make the most of life! You've worked hard—you've earned it. Money is not an object in itself, just a tool to help you accomplish other things. Lighten up! It'll add years to your life.

"When a person begins to think seriously of saving for a rainy day—it's probably a rainy day."

—Anonymous

Chapter 12

Making the most of your severance package

Using your RRSP

Severance or callback?

Strategies that help

The economy is booming, more people are working, consumer and corporate confidence is roaring along, and you've just been let go from your job. Unfortunately, it happens in the best of times, too. If you're a more senior employee, you could be forced into early retirement. But there are ways to handle these situations to minimize their effects on you, in the short term and long term.

Did you know . . .

. . . that the Bank of Montreal has forecast that Canada's unemployment rate will drop to 7.5% by 2001? It says that good times are looming for sectors such as electrical/electronic products, communications, machinery, aircraft and parts, motor vehicle assembly and parts, pipelines, and business services. Not looking as hospitable are the tobacco, forestry, wood, leather, and public service sectors.

The best possible place to stash the money you receive when you are laid off, fired, or just retired, is your RRSP. The rules allow termination or severance payments (technically called "retiring allowances") to be rolled over into an RRSP. If it is done directly by your former employer, no tax is withheld.

If you take a cheque (a really bad move) and then put the money in an RRSP, you will lose 30% in taxes—which you can claim back later on your tax return. However, you will also have lost precious time during which that sum could have been compounding tax-free in your RRSP. It's a hassle that you don't need right now.

MORE BAD NEWS

If you started working in 1996 or later, you are definitely out of luck when it comes to using this arrangement down the road. Finance Minister Paul Martin whacked it in his 1995 budget. Brutal. It's unfair and it should have been met with howls of protest when brought in, but it slipped through.

A lot of middle-class people have used this effective device to minimize the tax grab on their severance packages. But starting with the 1996 taxation year, it is eliminated for future years.

Since the ability to roll over money into a special spousal RRSP was ended after 1994, this had been one of the few ways to get funds over your annual contribution limit pumped into your retirement plan. (Other methods include an RRSP mortgage, marriage breakdown when assets are transferred, rollovers into a locked-in RRSP, and return of pension contribution plus interest into a non-locked-in plan.)

How much can I roll over?

For each year, or part of a year, prior to 1996 that you worked, you are eligible to put $2000 into your RRSP. In addition, you can contribute $1500 for each year prior to 1989 that you were not a part of the company's pension plan or deferred profit sharing plan. And the best part is that this amount does not count towards your personal contribution limit.

Eligible retiring allowance
(The amount of your severance package
you can shelter from tax)

$2000 × Years worked before 1996
+ $1500 × Years before 1989
without a company pension

For example, if you had worked for 25 years, were laid off this year, and were part of a company pension plan, you could put $46,000 into your RRSP (that's $2000 for the 23 years worked prior to 1996).

If you worked the same length of time and never contributed to a company pension plan, the eligible RRSP contribution would be $70,000 ($1500 for each of the 16 years worked prior to 1989 plus $2000 a year for the 23 years worked prior to 1996).

Now, with 1996 as the cut-off date, you will not be building up any additional rollover amount, but you will not (for now, at least) lose the amount you earned prior to that. For people just entering the work-force, of course, it means they will never be able to take advantage of tax-free retiring allowance.

STAYING AFLOAT

Now, everyone has financial commitments. If you can minimize these until a new work situation arises, you will not regret the sacrifice you make for a more comfortable retirement.

But sometimes life doesn't go according to plan, and withdrawals are necessary. If you need extra cash, you can withdraw up to $5000 from your RRSP and pay only 10% in tax. If you remove $5000 to $15,000, the rate goes up to 20%. In Quebec, the corresponding rates are 21% and 30%. RRSP withdrawals are treated the same as any other form of income. Therefore, your bank, credit union, trust company, or broker is required to withhold some of your withdrawal and send it to Ottawa.

Your financial adviser can provide immeasurable assistance to help you through this tumultuous time. Here are a few things to consider with RRSP withdrawals:

- Because the tax rate rises with the amount withdrawn, take money out in smaller amounts.
- Check on what limits your financial institution might have in place to discourage small RRSP withdrawals—a limit on the number of withdrawals you can make or special fees, for example.
- Claim any tax withheld on your income tax return.

TAX WITHHOLDING RATES

	Federal	Quebec
Up to $5,000	10%	21%
$5,000 to $15,000	20%	30%
Above $15,000	30%	35%

SOME GOOD NEWS

In the 1997 budget, the feds introduced a chance for you to recover lost RRSP contribution room if you were in a company pension plan and subject to the pension adjustment calculation. That means you can roll over your lump sum pension payout into your RRSP (again, don't take a cheque, just have the money transferred), and the lost RRSP room will be restored, minus the amount of the lump sum. This is all well and fine, but if you've just lost your job, there's not much of a chance you'll have the money to fill up that space right away. Be sure to use up that room, though, when you're back on your feet.

TAKE THE MONEY AND RUN

Or, at least have it shipped off to your RRSP. I'm often asked which is the best way to go if a person is laid off and offered a right of recall or a severance package. Every case is different. If it's a situation where seasonal layoffs are the norm, nine times out of ten, you're better off taking the package. This may be the only time in your working life when you get a nice lump sum to leverage up retirement assets.

You may be offered the chance to take over your accumulated pension contributions instead of leaving them where they are. This is usually a good idea. You and your financial adviser can probably invest this money to make it grow a lot faster.

For example, your package may offer you a $20,000 annual pension at age 65 or, instead, a commuted lump sum of $70,000. If you invested that money in a locked-in retirement account (LIRA) for 20 years at 10%, it could grow to give you a pension of $37,600 a year at age 65—a huge improvement! As well, when you die, your estate inherits your LIRA, which is better than a pension that expires when you do.

The decisions you make, of course, depend on your current financial status, monthly spending requirements, future prospects, and a discussion with your spouse and your financial adviser.

Did you know . . .

. . . that in the last year income was up by 2.3%? However, income taxes and other transfers to government rose by 6.2%. Personal spending was up by 5.7%. The result? A 1.8% personal savings rate, the worst seen since before the Second World War.

SOME VALUABLE TIPS TO REMEMBER:

- Ensure you get all that's coming to you. Any part of a year—even only one day—can qualify as a full year's amount.
- Part-time or seasonal work also qualifies, along with co-op job placements and internships.
- Make sure you carefully review your employment record before agreeing to a settlement package. Sometimes employers are unaware that a small part of a year worked can count as a full year on the job.
- Have your employer put the severance money directly into an RRSP for you; that way, you will not have withholding tax of up to 30% deducted right off the top.
- If you take the severance package, tax will be withheld. But, depending on how much of it you then put into an RRSP, you can get some or all of it back. Show the whole amount of the package on your income tax return at line 130 and then claim a deduction. Attach the RRSP receipt, or the claim will be disallowed.

- If the amount you are rolling over into your RRSP is huge, you may be nailed by the alternative minimum tax, set up to make sure that people making over $40,000 don't get enough tax deductions to reduce their income to zero. In this case, depending on when in the year you get the money, it may be smart to take the package over a couple of tax years.
- Are you self-employed? Then you have also built up eligible retirement allowance room over the years you paid yourself, and can roll over cash into your RRSP. And self-employed professionals who employ their spouses can give them a one-time retirement allowance payment when the business is being wound down.
- The retiring allowance RRSP rollover can go into your RRSP in the year it's received, or you can wait and do it in the first 60 days of the next year—depending on what's best for your tax profile.
- Finally, when you have lost your job and are offered a severance package, it is sometimes tempting to keep a portion in cash, instead of putting it away in an RRSP. Bad idea. You will lose up to a third of it in tax right off the top. Better to put it in an RRSP with no tax deducted and then remove what you need in small amounts ($5000 or less). That way, the withholding tax is only 10%.

As I have said many times in this book, talk to your financial adviser. If you suspect that you are in danger of losing your job, or have received notice, your adviser is best prepared to handle your severance and provide you with a plan to manage your period of unemployment—minimizing cash outflow, preventing depletion of your nest egg, and avoiding payment of more taxes than is necessary. On top of that, good luck.

"The inescapable conclusion was that to take money out of the future pension system at a time when the federal government will be running surpluses, simply seemed to be the wrong choice."

—Paul Martin, Federal Minister of Finance

Chapter 13

What will the government try next?

Five tax threats you need to know about

"Can you ever see a time when the government will tax RRSPs?" I get asked this a lot, especially at financial seminars. People are clearly worried about building up a highly visible nest egg that is vulnerable to attack by some future government.

The suspicion that there's a war on wealth in this country is shared by a lot of Canadians. And how can you blame them? Our top tax rate in this country is 15% higher than in the United States, and we start paying it at around the $60,000 mark while Americans don't get there until they earn well over $200,000.

Middle-aged, middle-class people probably have the most to lose over the next couple of decades. Today's retirees and those near retirement can count on government pension benefits. Younger generations are the most financially literate ever, and they have four decades to prepare. But the poor baby boomers 15 or 20 years from retirement, with far too little saved and struggling within a restructuring economy, are sitting ducks for more government revenue grabs.

But the threat of any future tax increases does not diminish the importance of RRSPs. Ottawa will continuously tinker with the rules, but I cannot foresee a major attack on personal retirement savings.

But there are clearly threats to the RRSP system. These, in my view, are the Big Five:

1. YOUR ABILITY TO CATCH UP ON MISSED CONTRIBUTIONS COULD END

As mentioned earlier, it's only a matter of time before the government puts a stop to this benefit. It might take another budget, or maybe five, but it's coming. There are over $200 billion in contributions that Canadians have missed making, but could easily catch up on if they employed some of the strategies in this book.

If they did, the government's books would easily swan-dive into the red thanks to all those rebate cheques and lost revenues. Keeping the budget balanced from here on in would be compromised to no end.

So, do not be surprised when the carry-forward provision is altered. It will either just be killed outright, with a return to pre-1991 rules—which said that you had to make your annual contribution or lose it—or we'll go back to allowing a carry-forward for a defined number of years.

> ***If you have a carry-forward today, use it. If you lack the cash, borrow it. If you have other assets, make a contribution in kind. Any delay is a gamble you need not take.***

2. RRSP CONTRIBUTIONS COULD BECOME TAX CREDITS, NOT DEDUCTIONS

This would be sneaky—which means it's not above any government—and a heck of an effective way for the feds to reduce the revenue lost due to the current system. Today, you are allowed to deduct the whole amount of your RRSP contribution from your taxable income. That directly reduces the amount of tax you pay and, in fact, **the more money you make, the more taxes you save.**

Right now, people in the top tax bracket get back 53 cents on every dollar they contribute to their retirement plan, compared with 25 cents on the dollar for people earning less than $30,000.

Source: Financial Post

If the contribution was treated as a credit, the refund for lower income earners would remain about the same, but it would tumble for those making more. Those in the top tax bracket would see that 53-cent tax break fall to about 30 cents—reducing the tax benefit by about half.

An attempt, a few years ago, to go this route was thwarted as Bill C-364 bit the dirt. That doesn't mean we've seen the end of this meddling. Be ready to howl if this tinkering is revived.

> **Did you know . . .**
> . . . if the Seniors Benefit had become law, Ottawa would have stripped about $8 billion annually from pension payments? This, at the height of the baby boom retirement bulge in 2030.

3. RRSP ASSETS COULD BE TAXED DIRECTLY

This idea has already been floated by Jim Peterson, when he was chairman of the House of Commons finance committee. He raised the trial balloon before the federal budget was brought down a couple of years ago but, to his credit, Finance Minister Paul Martin didn't take the bait.

What Peterson mused on was a 1% annual tax on RRSPs with more than $500,000 in them. Politically, that has curb appeal, because half a million sounds like a lot of money and 1% sounds like a very small tax.

But the implications are horrific. Such a tax would seriously compromise the whole intent of the system, erode investor confidence, and rattle the financial markets. It would break faith with taxpayers and signal that the government simply cannot be trusted with long-term fiscal and social policy.

That, of course, is no reason it couldn't happen. But even such a backward and myopic move by the federal government would not overcome the advantages of contributing heavily to an RRSP.

4. CONTRIBUTION LEVELS COULD BE SLASHED AGAIN

They already have been—several times, in fact. The old rules said we should be at an annual level of $15,500 by now. But here we are, frozen at a maximum of $13,500 well into the new century.

Today's rules still say that the limit will be raised higher when the current freeze ends, and eventually will be indexed to inflation. But don't bet your spouse on it. Only a tiny percentage of Canadians actually qualify to make the top contribution, so dropping it would not have major consequences and would send out the desired political signal that rich layabouts have to pay more.

5. THE TIME YOU HAVE LEFT TO SAVE COULD BE CUT

This has already started, of course. The 1996 budget reduced the age at which you can no longer contribute to your RRSP by two years, from 71 to 69.

The implications of that are large. It removed from everyone the potential to shelter from tax tens of thousands of dollars. It shaved 24 months off of the time you could have added assets to your plan. And it accelerated by the same time the date at which you have to start collapsing your savings.

Now that the age has been changed once, it can be changed again. In fact, it's possible that the RRSP contribution cut-off age and the official retirement age might soon be the same—say, 67.

AND THE ANSWER IS . . .

Let me make it clear: These are just possibilities. I have no hard evidence that any of these threats will come to pass, but then, nobody expected the 1996 budget to attack RRSPs as it did. Ironically, one of the most forward-thinking things the federal government can do is to encourage more private savings and future financial independence. The best way of dealing with the coming retirement crisis is to allow Canadians to build their savings. And the best tool for that is, yes, the RRSP.

If you agree, don't be shy about saying so. Let the powers that be know about your displeasure. It helped waylay the Seniors Benefit. So nothing is impossible. Here's your MP's address: House of Commons, Ottawa, ON K1A 0A6. You don't even need to use a stamp.

Chapter 14

Why everybody needs an adviser

The greatest financial mistake you can make is thinking you do not need help. Of course you need help. We all do. And while I hope this book has expanded your knowledge of the investment choices available, it is no substitute for a trusted adviser who knows you and your goals.

We all face the same dilemma—interest rates are too low to allow you to be conservative in your investments. You know your life will be very long and expensive. And yet investing for growth means facing up to risk—considerable risk. Are you comfortable making these decisions alone? Have you learned enough about all the possible options and dangers? Can you find the time necessary to research everything?

Well, I can't. So I rely heavily on my adviser—a person I trust to make the right decisions at the right time, when I'm on the road or focusing on making some money (rather than managing it).

Most Canadians are gambling horribly with their financial futures because they entrust their money entirely to rank amateurs with no formal training who devote, on average, about two hours a year to the job and refuse to consider any research or investment information that isn't free. That's right—they try to do their own financial planning. Big, big mistake. Consider this:

- Six in 10 Canadians believe they will not have $250,000 in net worth on the day they retire, according to a Gallup poll. It is shocking evidence of how unprepared Canadians are for what lies ahead. Even with public pensions in place, these folks are likely to see a drastic drop in their standard of living in retirement.
- Record numbers of people have been going bankrupt, even as interest rates and unemployment decline.
- The national savings rate hit zero in 1999. Household debt levels continue to climb.
- Too many Canadians have too much of their net worth locked up in one type of asset that has been declining in value for most of the decade—residential real estate.
- About two-thirds of Canadians made an RRSP contribution in 1999. Most taxpayers have no idea that with one phone call they can open an RRSP with no cash and transfer into it things they already own.
- Collectively Canadians are about $200 billion behind in RRSP contributions.
- Most people think that Canada Savings Bonds provide an excellent long-term return, when they actually wither as an investment. Only a quarter of the people with bond or mortgage mutual funds know that those funds will fall when interest rates rise. Worse still, only 14% of people can identify the best-performing investment class since the Second World War. Of course, it's stocks.
- Crazed investors sold hundreds of millions of dollars worth of mutual funds in the last three trading days before the Quebec referendum of October 1995—just after the TSE 300 had been clobbered and fund values reduced. The day after the referendum, most people bought the funds back—at higher prices.
- People clamour to buy investments at their highest value and dump them when they fall. Remember the folks lined up in Toronto to buy gold at $1000 an ounce? Today the metal is worth a third of that. How about those who bought $1-million homes on a nice street north of Toronto in 1989? Years later, half that street was for sale at $500,000 a house. And recall how many investors bailed after Black Monday 1987, and then missed one of the greatest run-ups in stock market history?

Source: The Globe and Mail

- Millions of Canadians keep billions of dollars in low-yield GICs when they could be earning returns with less risk in other securities—because they've never heard of seg funds, strip bonds, or mortgage-backed securities.

Be wary of the bad apples

News about unethical advisers has not been hard to find in the news. In Ontario, a top-producing mutual fund salesman was banned for life after pocketing secret payments and leaving his clients with worthless investments. Two of the country's top mutual fund managers lost their jobs over personal actions; one was even banned for six months from trading. In Toronto, a financial adviser stole more than $800,000 from the accounts of three elderly clients, including a defenseless woman with Alzheimer Disease.

Yes, some people have been ripped off by unscrupulous financial advisers. Some advisers turn out to be churners—excessively buying and selling investments just to maximize commissions, at the expense of the client's portfolio. Others are just cheats. Some "top producers" at rapidly growing financial services companies get there not by making wise investments but rather by racing through legions of clients.

You are right to approach this exercise with caution, but not with cynicism or scepticism. The simple truth is that almost everyone would be better off with a personal financial adviser. The key is to find someone with knowledge and integrity. The good news is that there are many to choose from, and the vast majority of individuals I have worked with over the years at seminars across the country are simply outstanding.

Here are my answers to the questions I'm most often asked about finding an adviser you can trust:

How do I know if an adviser is qualified? Are there regulations?

People who sell financial securities have to be licensed. But the industry, as a whole, is unregulated, which means that finding a good adviser is going to take some work on your part. The Canadian Association of Financial Planners has about 1600 members, accounting for just 20% of all people who call themselves planners. There are currently no national standards, but there are a few designations to consider.

"Registered Financial Planner" or RFP is the designation given by the Canadian Association of Financial Planners. "Chartered Financial Planner" or CFP designates someone who's completed the correspondence course of the Canadian Association of Insurance and Financial Advisers (CAIFA). "Chartered Life Underwriter" or CLU is the stamp of approval from CAIFA.

To further confuse things, the Canadian Association of Financial Planners and the Life Underwriters have teamed up to create the Financial Planners Standards Council of Canada (FPSCC), which promotes yet another designation, the "Certified Financial Planner," or CFP. It looks like this last one may turn out to be the industry norm, since that term is already recognized in the United States and a few other countries.

Meanwhile, the people who train bankers and stock brokers pulled out of the FPSCC in 1998. So, here are some other designations to look for: a "Certified Investment Manager," or CIM, is sanctioned by the Canadian Securities Institute, while the Institute of Canadian Bankers stands behind the designations of "Personal Financial Planner," or PFP, and "Specialist in Financial Counselling," or SFC.

Confusing? Yes. So just ask the advisers your are interviewing for a summary of their education and special training and, of course, their experience and references.

What does good advice cost?

Most people think that a financial planner will charge a huge amount of money. Usually, that's not the case. In fact, most planners work for you for free. The right way to think about most planners is the same way you think about travel agents—you can get your ticket to Montreal and pay Air Canada $500, or your travel agent can arrange it, and it still costs $500.

That's because Air Canada will do a lot more business each year with your agent than with you, and so the airline is happy to pay the agent a commission—in effect, lowering the cost of the ticket.

Your financial planner is paid a commission by the mutual fund company or bond issuer or the insurance company when you add that investment to your portfolio. Of course, you can hire an adviser who is fee-only and does not actually arrange for any investments to be made. That will cost you up to $2000 for a complete financial plan and an hourly consultation fee ranging from $50 to $250, with most in the $100 area. Then, you will still need someone to implement the plan and purchase the securities.

You will often see "expert" opinion in the media warning you away from commission-paid advisers and into the arms of fee-paid ones. Ignore this. For the vast majority of people who have under $1 million in liquid assets, an adviser who is remunerated through commissions is just fine.

What can you expect? For starters, a free 60- to 90-minute consultation. From there, the adviser prepares an analysis of your assets and drafts a financial plan and recommendations. Typically, it costs you nothing—so what possible excuse could you have for not getting a valuable second opinion on how you're doing?

Eight Common Investor Mistakes an Adviser Can Help You Avoid

- Waiting for the "best" time to invest, or never investing
- Buying at a high price, selling at a low one
- Buying yesterday's hot investment
- Choosing investments not suited to individual goals or time horizons
- Failing to diversify
- Reacting to short-term events rather than long-term trends
- Basing investment decisions on fees and sales charges
- Basing investment decisions on emotions rather than facts

Source: Mutual Fund Forum

Where do I start?

Ask others who they use as advisers—word-of-mouth references are good because you can get a feel for an adviser's track record from somebody you know.

Naturally, you can respond to ads published in the financial section of your local newspaper—especially during RRSP season when lots of them offer particular investments.

Better still, go to a few financial seminars. Most are free, and during RRSP season and tax time there are a number to choose from. A great deal of information can be had in a short period of time, and the financial planners hosting them invariably offer anyone who attends a free consultation.

But a word of caution: Not all seminars are what they appear to be. Some are come-ons for expensive and needless courses on no-money-down real estate or sure-thing business opportunities. So, if you go to one, leave your chequebook at home.

Just listen and you can quickly determine if this is a sales pitch—with one or two specific investment products being hyped—or the introduction of a useful service and an adviser who sounds promising.

What questions should I ask?

During that first meeting, the adviser will ask for a lot of information on your income, assets, taxes, family situation, and goals. In return, you should ask about how that person expects to be paid, areas of personal expertise, and their track record and credentials. Be tough. Be frank. Be candid. Ask where the adviser puts his or her own money, why, and what the results have been.

Ask about his or her investment philosophy. Does it match yours? Are you being offered more than just a family of mutual funds? Are you getting advice tailored specifically to your situation?

Here's a list of questions American investors are urged to ask of a potential planner, published in the *Wall Street Journal*. These are good questions to start with:

Things You Should Ask Advisers During Interviews

- What is your area of expertise?
- What is your approach to saving and investing?
- Will you provide an individualized financial plan?
- What kinds of communications are sent on an ongoing basis (account statements, newsletters)?
- How often will you review my portfolio?
- How are you compensated for the service you provide?
- How are fees calculated?
- On average, how much can I expect to pay for your service?
- What do I receive in return for that fee?
- What, if anything, do you expect of me during our relationship?

Should I ask for references?

Absolutely. In fact, this is the most important thing to ask for. A good adviser has nothing to hide. In fact, a good adviser will be proud of his or her clients' success, and will want to share it with you.

So ask for a list of 10 or 12 people they have worked with. Then call and ask for a candid appraisal of the planner's effectiveness. Has the adviser reduced their tax bill? Increased their net worth? Diversified their investments? What overall rate of return are they getting on their portfolios? How often do they hear from the adviser? Are they kept fully informed? Are they concerned about excessive trading in their accounts? Are they related to the adviser (it does happen!)?

What level of service should I expect?

Several meetings at first to approve an investment and tax strategy, then regular updates—perhaps quarterly. Your portfolio should be reviewed several times a year, or as changing conditions dictate.

You should get a regular account statement—monthly is best—and it should break down all transactions, giving rates of return and securities held along with weightings by asset class (for example, 41% mutual funds, 32% fixed income, 27% equities).

Many good advisers provide clients with newsletters, access to investment research, or client appreciation nights at which investment professionals come to speak. Advisers with some of the larger investment firms also are backed by substantial research departments along with access to new stock and bond offerings.

The most important thing to expect is a comfortable working relationship with somebody you trust.

How can I tell if it's not working?

A tell-tale sign you're working with the wrong person is churning. That's when the adviser is buying and selling a lot of mutual fund units or stocks for no good reason other than to earn more in commission.

What's the difference between a planner, a broker, and a counsellor?

Many planners work for companies that offer a full range of financial products, including strip bonds, stocks, mutual funds, GICs, and more. These planners usually earn their living through commissions paid by funds and other companies. Most will be happy to tell you exactly who pays them, and how much they are.

A broker is licensed to sell any financial product and must have completed the Canadian Securities Course. He or she will work for a brokerage company regulated by the Investment Dealers Association of Canada. A broker also earns money through commissions on every transaction.

An investment counsellor is paid through fees that can take the form of an annual payment or a percentage of the total portfolio under management. Usually counsellors are the preserve of the rich—those with more than $500,000 in investible assets. They, by the way, account for only 1.6% of the population.

How do I know if an adviser is full-service?

Ask. Some planners only sell mutual funds, so obviously they will not be able to give your portfolio the required balance and diversity. You want an adviser who will look at your total financial picture—real estate, insurance, estate, tax, and investment plans.

What about discount brokers?

These are no-frills operations that allow you to buy stocks, bonds, or funds at a vastly cheaper commission cost than with a full-service broker or planner. Examples are T-D's impressive Waterhouse operation and the Royal Bank's Action Direct. Discount brokers are innovative and cutting-edge in terms of the latest investor technology. Canada Trust, Action Direct, and Waterhouse all offer real-time trading via personal computer, as do E-trade, Charles Schwab and others—an experience that can get any person's adrenalin pumping.

The downside is the same as for no-load mutual funds—no help. The people on the phone or the modem line are order-takers, not experienced investment advisers. The discounters also don't publish research, send out newsletters, or call with new Initial Public Offerings (IPOs). But if you know what you want and are determined to save money on commissions—and accept the risk of a making a bad decision—then go for it.

Should I go with a small company or a big one?

There is no right answer to this question, because it is the individual adviser that really matters. The advantage of a small office or firm is that you stand a better chance of getting personal. But the advantage of a large firm is access to research and a full range of investment options. My personal recommendation would be to find a small office of a big company. That way you can establish a close relationship with the people working there and still enjoy the benefits accorded clients of the busiest downtown mega-operation.

Always remember: A good financial adviser is more interested in a long-term relationship than in making quick commissions. As your wealth grows, so does the adviser's compensation—so over a 15- or 20-year period, your financial well-being is your adviser's main concern.

Should I give over all my money?

Probably not—at least, not at first. You need to build a relationship and see your adviser at work. So, don't write a cheque representing your life savings right off the bat. But, by the same token, don't hand over $5000 and expect to see dramatic results in a few weeks

Once you feel comfortable with the advice you are getting, it does make sense to consolidate your portfolio with one person. That way you can achieve diversity, organize the best tax planning strategies, and ensure the right mix of assets for your stage of life and risk tolerance.

Here's how to reach me

Why not come out to one of my financial seminars, and meet some planners? Follow it up with a consultation, and make up your own mind. If you'd like the names of some advisers that I might know in your area, send me a fax or an e-mail. Last year, about 8,000 people did! You can access my current seminar schedule through my Internet Web site. Here's how to reach me:

- By phone: (416) 489-2188
- By fax: (416) 489-2189
- By e-mail: garth@garth.ca
- On the World Wide Web: http://www.garth.ca
- By mail: Garth Turner
Suite 310, 1670 Bayview Ave.,
Toronto, Ont. M4G 3C2

Access to the internet shifts power to the financial product end-user by removing dependence on advisers and brokers.

—Colleen Moorehead, President,
Versus Brokerage Services Inc.
(www.canada.etrade.com)

Chapter 15

Resources

INFO ON THE NET:

Financial advisers
Financial planning software
Retirement planning
Tax planning
Tax preparation
Accounting firms
Full-service brokers
Stock quotes
Stock trading
Stock information
Mutual funds
Investment advice
Publications & newsletters
Web search engines
Funds by phone

HOOKED ON THE NET

You can use the Internet to shop for a financial planner, buy mutual fund units, get free financial advice, and access the brightest minds at the country's top accounting and pension consulting firms. The amount of information available is daunting. No, it is overwhelming. You can drown in the stuff.

Besides, it changes by the hour with new Web sites being created and loaded up with material. I have no doubt that by the time these words are printed and in your hands that there will be more excellent offerings on the World Wide Web and other areas of the Internet. All you have to do is conduct a net search using the words "investment" or "retirement" and thousands of entries will appear before you.

If you do not have a computer or access to the Internet, don't worry: Simply finding a good financial adviser is all the help that 99% of Canadians need. But if you do have access to the Internet, and are willing to devote a few hours to comparing sites, here are some to check out. Most of these you will find linked to my own Web site, along with banks, government resources, economics departments, news organizations, and others.

My Web site address is www.garth.ca.

Financial advisers

Regional contact names and phone numbers for the Canadian Association of Financial Planners are listed on one Web site, which also has areas explaining the basics of financial planning and even offers answers to your questions by e-mail. It also has a good checklist on how to find a financial adviser and planning tips.

Canadian Association of Financial Planners
www.cafp.org

As well, The Fund Library's site, which is getting about 50,000 hits a day, has the online résumés of about a hundred investment advisers.

The Fund Library
www.fundlib.com/ibd

Financial planning software

A superior site for financial planning, mutual fund information, and links to an astounding number of companies, resources, and individual financial planners is the one run by The Fund Library. You can also join a discussion group on mutual fund strategies. And it offers free financial planning software, including Trimark's interactive educational program.

The Fund Library
www.fapages.com

Retirement planning

Many sites are available, and the two mentioned above have links to several of them. Perhaps the best is RetireWeb, which is packed with information and run by actuary Scott Parkinson, complete with separate areas for people who are retired, nearly retired, or years from it. Access government programs from here and use the powerful calculators to determine retirement income needs or whether you should be paying your mortgage off instead of making RRSP contributions. It does everything except tell you how long you'll live.

RetireWeb
www.retireweb.com

Diamond Retirement Planning Ltd.
www.diamondretirement.com

Canadian Association of Retired Persons
www.fifty-plus.com

These are other good sites for retired seniors to browse.

Bank of Montreal's Retire Right Page
www.bmo.com

Merrill Lynch
www.canada.ml.com

Money Magazine
www.iemoney.com

The Mutual Group
www.themutualgroup.com

Nesbitt Burns Personal Finance Pages
www.nesbittburns.com

Seniors Computer Information Project
www.crm.mb.ca

TD Bank's Canadian Home Income Plan
www.chip.ca

Tax planning

One good place to start is Revenue Canada's Web site, which offers instant online access to all those guides and brochures that can take forever to get by mail. It also lists the latest tax rulings and changes, along with RevCan initiatives that are useful to know about.

Revenue Canada
www.rc.gc.ca

Tax preparation

While I think most people are either cheap or delusional to prepare their own income tax returns, there's little doubt that some good tax-return software will help cut down on the errors. Here are three to sample:

CanTax
www.cantax.com

TaxPrep
www.taxprep.com

Tax Wiz
www.taxstuff.com

Accounting firms

Believe it or not, Canada's largest accounting firms are innovative, aggressive, and incredibly useful sources of information on the Internet. They offer the best analysis of federal and provincial budgets and even have interactive question-and-answer areas where you can access a tax professional. You can also download current tax tables and calculate your tax liability.

Ernst & Young
www.eycan.com

Grant Thornton
www.grantthornton.ca

KPMG
www.kpmg.ca

Deloitte & Touche
www.deloitte.ca

PriceWaterhouseCoopers
www.pwcglobal.com

Full-service brokers

Whether it's an online brochure, analytical research, or information such as account status, here's how you can connect with some of the bigger players in the field.

CIBC Wood Gundy Securities
www.cibcwg.com

Merrill Lynch
www.canada.ml.com

Nesbitt Burns Inc.
www.nesbittburns.com

RBC Dominion
www.rbcds.com

Scotia Capital Markets
www.scotiacapital.com

Online brokers

There are firms that offer stock trading on the Internet. This is probably the least expensive way possible to execute a trade—as low as US$14.95. Here are a few sites to look at:

Aufhauser & Co.
www.aufhauser.com

E-Trade Canada
www.etrade.com

E.Schwab Online Investing
www.schwab.com

Green Line
www.greenline.ca

Investor Line
www.investorline.com

Lombard Institutional Brokerage
www.lombard.com

Stock quotes

It is now possible to get real-time stock quotes, buy securities online, and get instant access to high-quality and current charts and graphs of stock performance—once the stuff reserved for the eyes of stockbrokers only. Several of these sites also provide powerful calculators and links to major U.S. financial sites.

Quote.com
www.quote.com

Security APL Quote Service
www.secapl.com

Stockmaster
www.stockmaster.com

Canadian Stock Market Reporter
www.canstock.com

CT Securities International Inc.
www.ctsecurities.com

PC Quote Inc.
www.pcquote.on.ca

NETWorth
www.networth.galt.com

Telescan
www.telescan.com

InterQuote
www.interquote.com

Montreal Stock Exchange
www.me.com

Vancouver Stock Exchange
www.vse.com

Alberta Stock Exchange
www.alberta.net

Nasdaq Stock Market
www.nasdaq.com

American Stock Exchange
www.amex.com

Chicago Merchantile Exchange
www.cme.com

Holt's Market Report
www.holtreport.com

Stock trading

There are currently no Canadian investment firms that offer stock trading on the Internet, but Toronto Dominion Bank's innovative Green Line Investment Services will likely be the first. But there are several ways to trade U.S. stocks, in what is a direct challenge to traditional stock exchanges. This is probably the least expensive way possible to execute a trade—as low as US$14.95.

E-Trade Securities
www.canada.etrade.com

E.Schwab Online Investing
www.schwab.com

Lombard Institutional Brokerage
www.lombard.com

Aufhauser & Co.
www.aufhauser.com

Stock information

The first and only real-time news release database is Canada Stockwatch, which provides all the news releases for all Canadian public companies. That means it has over 400,000 releases, giving invaluable amounts of information on companies in which you might want to buy stocks.

Canada Stockwatch
www.canada-stockwatch.com

StockPoint
www.imet.com

StockSmart
www.stocksmart.com

Mutual funds

The fund companies have taken to the Internet in a big way, and some of the sites are comprehensive—and getting a lot of traffic. Many of these offer daily newsbriefing services, overviews of the equity and bond markets, fund quotes, links to American sites, performance graphs, economics reports, and much more. Of course, they contain extensive information on the various funds offered. It pays to surf before you buy.

One site bears special mention for its huge library of links to others financial sites, including all major mutual funds, search engines, news sources, stock and mutual fund quotes, precious metals Web sites, and more—thanks to the Royal Bank.

Royal Mutual Funds
www.royalbank.com

Here are the other major Canadian mutual fund locations, listed alphabetically:

AGF Group
www.agf.com

AIC
www.aicfunds.com

Altamira
www.altamira.com

BOM First Canadian Fund
www.bom.com

BPI
www.bpi.com

CIBC Funds
www.cibc.com

Canada Trust
www.canadatrust.com

C.I. Mutual Funds
www.cifunds.com

Dynamic Mutual Funds
www.dynamic.ca

Elliot & Page
www.fundlib.com

Fidelity Investments
www.fidelity.ca

G.T. Global
www.gtglobal.ca

Investors Group
www.investorsgroup.com

Mackenzie Financial
www.mackenziefinancial.com

Sagit Investment
www.direct.ca

Scotia Mutual
www.scotiabank.ca

Scudder Canada
www.scudder.ca

Spectrum United Mutual Funds
www.spectrumunited.com

Talvest
www.talvest.com

Templeton Canada
www.templeton.ca

TD Mutual Funds
www.tdbank.ca

Trimark Investment Management
www.trimark.com

Investment advice, publications, and newsletters

Here are some sites I have visited that offer reams of information on investment trends, high-tech stocks, financial gossip and insider reports, corporate profiles, and more.

Canadian Ethical Investment
www.web.net/ethmoney

Canadian Financial Network Inc.
www.canadianfinance.com

Canadian Online Explore
www.canoe.ca

Cannex Financial Exchanges Inc.
www.cannex.com

Fundata Canada Inc.
www.fundata.com

Good Money
www.goodmoney.com

InvestAlert Online
www.investalert.com

Investment Funds Institute of Canada
www.ific.ca

Mutual Funds Interactive
www.fundsinteractive.com

Portfolio Analytics
www.pal.com

Pristine Day Trader
www.pristine.com

IBC Financial Data
www.ibcdata.com

The Newsletter Library
http://pub.savvy.com

The Silicon Investor
www.techstocks.com

Barron's Magazine
www.barrons.com

Money Magazine
www.moneymag.com

Bloomberg Business News
www.bloomberg.com

Web search engines

These are simply devices to help you find more related sites on the Internet. You can find search engines in countless place on the World Wide Web, but three of the main ones—Webcrawler, Yahoo!, and Lycos—are on the Investment Funds Institute of Canada site, along with links to mutual funds, industry information, and a glossary of investment terms.

Investment Funds Institute of Canada
www.mutfunds.com/ific

Thomson Financial Publishing FINdex
www.findex.com

Alta Vista Web
www.altavista.digital.com

My belief is that the Internet will become the primary source of financial information in the years to come. The day is already here when you can do all of your banking and investing from a home computer. Just a couple of years ago no major Canadian financial institution was on the Internet—today, they are competing vigorously in cyberspace. For the average investor, this is incredibly empowering.

We now have access to more information than has ever been offered before. The trick is to wade through and find what is of true value. Just as it is overwhelming to walk through a large library trying to comprehend what lies in each volume, so the Internet is of no use unless mapped, charted, and bookmarked.

If you come across Web sites and Internet addresses you feel could help other RRSP investors, please let me know and I will endeavour to get that information in next year's edition of this guide.

FUNDS BY PHONE

If you're still trying to figure out how to program the VCR, then perhaps you're not ready for surfing the Internet just yet. Here's how you can contact most of the major fund companies by using basic technology, our old standby, the telephone:

ABC Funds	416-365-9696
Arcadia Investment Funds Inc.	800-351-1345
AGF Management Ltd.	800-268-8583
AIC Limited	800-263-2144 (Ont.)
AIM Fund Group of Canada	800-667-2369
All-Canadian Management	905-648-2025
Allstar Fund Group Ltd.	800-822-6446
Altamira Management Ltd.	800-263-2824 (Ont.)
AMI Private Capital	416-865-1985
Associate Investors Ltd.	416-864-1120
Atlas Asset Management Inc.	800-463-2857
Bank of Bermuda (Global Manager Funds)	441-299-5600
Bank of Montreal Inv. Mgmt. Ltd.	416-927-6000
B.E.S.T. Discoveries Fund	800-465-1812
Beutel Goodman Managed Funds	800-461-4551
Bissett & Associates Investments	403-266-4664
BNP (Canada) Inc.	514-285-2920
BPI Mutual Funds	800-263-2427
Burgeonvest Investment Counsel	905-528-6505
Caldwell Securities Ltd.	416-862-7755
Canada Life Assurance Co.	800-387-4447
Canada Trust	800-668-8888
Canadian Anaesthetists Mutual Accum.	800-267-4713
Capital Alliance Management Inc.	800-304-2330
Capstone Consultants Ltd.	416-863-0005
Cassels Blaikie & Co. Ltd.	416-941-7500

Canadian Dental Association	800-591-9401
Canadian Venture Opportunities Fund	888-527-4811
Century DJ Fund	416-608-0727
Chou Associates Management Inc.	416-299-6749
C.I. Mutual Funds	800-563-5181
CIBC Securities Inc.	800-465-3863
Clarington Capital Management Inc.	888-860-9888
Clean Environment Mutual Funds	800-461-4570
Colonia Life Insurance Co.	800-463-9297
Confederation Life Insurance Co.	902-453-4300
Co-operators Life Insurance Co.	800-667-8164
Corp. Financiers Du St-Laurent	514-288-7545
Cote 100 Inc.	800-454-2683 (Que.)
CSA Management Ltd.	800-363-3463
Deacon Capital Corporation	416-350-3232
DGC Entertainment Ventures Corp.	800-EVC-1159
Dominion Equity Resource Fund	403-531-2657
Dynamic Mutual Funds	800-268-8186
Elliott & Page Ltd.	800-363-6647
The Empire Life Insurance Co.	613-548-1881
The Enterprise Fund	800-563-3857
Equitable Life Insurance Co. of Canada	800-387-0588
Ethical Funds Inc.	800-267-5019
Fidelity Investments Canada Ltd.	800-263-4077
Fiducie Desjardins	800-361-2680
First Horizon Capital Corp.	800-665-1158
First Marathon Securities Ltd.	800-661-FUND
First Ontario LSIF Ltd.	800-777-7506
Fonds des Professionels du Quebec	800-363-6713
Friedberg Commodity Management Inc.	800-461-2700
GBC Asset Management Inc.	800-668-7383
Gentrust Investment Counsellors	800-341-1419
Global Strategy Financial Inc.	800-387-1229
GlobeInvest Funds Management Inc.	800-387-0784
Gordon Daly Grenadier Securities	800-268-9165
Great-West Life Assurance Co.	800-665-0049
G.T. Global Canada Inc.	800-588-5684
Guardian Group of Funds	800-668-7327
Guardian Timing Services Inc.	416-960-4890
Hongkong Bank Securities Inc.	800-830-8888
Howson Tattersall Investment Counsel	888-287-2966

HRL Investment Funds	800-268-9622
Imperial Life Assurance Co. (Can)	416-324-1617
Industrial Alliance Life Ins. Co.	800-268-8882
Integra Capital Management Corp.	416-367-0404
InvesNat Mutual Funds	800-363-3511
Investors Group	888-746-6344
John D. Hillery Counsel Inc.	416-234-0846
Jones Heward Investment Mgmt. Inc.	800-361-1392
Laurentian Bank Investment Services	416-865-5832
Le Fonds de Solidarite des Travailleurs du Quebec (FTQ)	800-361-5017
Leith Wheeler Management	604-683-3391
London Life Insurance Co.	519-432-5281
Loring Ward Investment Counsel Ltd.	800-267-1730
Lutheran Life Ins. Society of Canada	800-563-6237
M.K. Wong & Associates	800-665-9360
Mackenzie Financial Corporation	800-387-0615
Majendie Securities Ltd.	604-682-6446
Managed Investments Ltd.	800-287-5211
Mandate Management Corp.	604-731-2899
Manulife Financial	416-229-4515
Manulife Securities International Ltd.	800-265-7401
Maritime Life Assurance Co.	902-453-4300
Mawer Investment Management	403-262-4673
Maxxum Group of Funds	888-4-MAXXUM
McDonald Financial Corporation	416-594-1979
McLean Budden Limited	416-862-9800
MD Management Ltd.	800-267-4022
Metropolitan Life Insurance Ltd.	800-267-9375
Middlefield Resource Management Ltd.	416-362-0714
MOF Management Ltd.	800-663-6370
Montrusco Associates Inc.	514-842-6464
Morrison Williams Investment Mgmt.	416-777-2922
Mutual Investco Inc.	519-888-FUND
National Life of Canada	800-242-9753
National Trust Co.	800-563-4683
Navigator Fund Company, Ltd.	800-665-1667
NN Life Insurance of Canada	416-391-2200
North-West Life Ins. Co. of Canada	604-689-1211
O'Donnell Investment Mgmt. Corp.	800-292-5658
OHA Investment Management Ltd.	800-268-9597

Ontario Teachers Group Inc.	800-263-9541
Optimum Placements Inc.	888-678-4686
Orbit World Fund	514-932-3000
Pacific Capital Management Ltd.	800-662-5338
Peter Cundhill & Associates Ltd.	800-663-0156
Phillips, Hager & North Investment Mgmt.	800-661-6141
Primerica Life Ins. Co. of Canada	800-387-7876
Prosperity Capital Corporation	416-867-3863
Pucetti Funds Management Inc.	905-649-5588
Pursuit Financial Management Corp.	800-253-9619
Retrocom Growth Fund Inc.	888-743-5627
Royal Bank Investment Mgmt. Inc.	800-463-3863
Royal Life Canada	800-263-1747
Royal Trust	800-463-3863
Sagit Management Ltd.	800-663-1003
Sceptre Investment Counsel Ltd.	800-265-1888
Scotia Securities Inc.	800-268-9269
Scudder Funds of Canada	800-850-3863
Seaboard Life Insurance Company	800-363-2166
Societe Financiere Azura Inc.	800-231-6539
Spectrum United Mutual Funds Inc.	800-263-1851
Sportfund Inc.	800-970-SPORT
Standard Life	800-665-6237
Standard Life Mutual Funds Ltd.	800-665-6237
Stone & Co. Limited	800-336-9528
Strategic Value Funds Mgmt. Inc.	800-408-2311
Talvest Fund Management Inc.	800-268-8258
Templeton International Ltd.	800-387-0830
Toronto-Dominion Asset Management	800-268-8166
Tradex Management Inc.	800-567-FUND
Transamerica Life Ins. Co. of Canada	416-290-2818
Triax Growth Fund Inc.	800-407-0287
Trimark Investment Management Inc.	800-387-9845
Trust General du Canada	800-280-3088
Trust Pret & Revenu	800-667-7643
University Avenue Management	800-465-1812
Valorem Inc.	888-922-5622
Value Contrarian Asset Management	514-398-0808
Westbury Canadian Life Insurance Co.	800-263-9241
Working Opportunity Fund	604-688-9631
Working Ventures Canadian Fund	800-268-8244

The Turner Report

THE BEST DEFENCE: KNOWLEDGE

The Turner Report is Canada's fastest-growing personal finance newsletter.

"I just wanted to say thanks for *The Turner Report*. Since subscribing, I have followed your advice and done extremely well by it."

C.O.
@home.com

"I am enjoying *The Turner Report* very much. It's Canadian content, it's very interesting, with good strategies and timely information, and last, but not least, from a fellow boomer—what more can I say? Keep up the great work."

D.M.
Sault Ste. Marie, Ontario

"My wife and I are recent subscribers to *The Turner Report* and enjoy the monthly financial information we receive. Every issue is most informative."

D.P.
Sandilands, Manitoba

"Keep up the good work of telling the truth and helping the ordinary investor to become a contributing citizen of this great country of ours."

D.B.
@aol.com

The Turner Report is a monthly newsletter that will give you an update of this book, the best investment advice I can find, and answers to the questions that must be answered.

Y2K. Deflation. Wild markets. Asia. Weird weather. The threats are obvious, and many people are paralysed by them. But at the same time, others are amassing personal wealth as never before. Have you seen the new Mercedes on the streets of Vancouver and Calgary? The bidding wars for million-dollar houses in Toronto? While at the same time, government numbers prove that most people's incomes have gone down during the last decade of the millennium.

The gap is widening between those on the top and those straining to hold on to the middle. It's also a gap between savers and investors—those with their money in the wrong kinds of assets are losing ground fast.

Most Canadians don't have an RRSP. Most have no company pension. The public pension plan is in jeopardy—we will contribute more to it and get less in return. Does this sound like a recipe for retirement disaster? You bet. But if you follow at least some of the strategies in this book, you should be better off than most people.

But, as I have also shown, for those people who realize where we are right now in the economic cycle, who see the fundamental shift from real assets to financial assets, who properly use the equity in their homes, and who understand the actions of the worried baby boomers over the next decade and a half, this is a time of unbridled opportunity.

- You can borrow $50,000 or $100,000 with a phone call, or a click of a mouse, at an effective rate of less than 4%.

- You can invest to earn double-digit rates of return in quality investment funds.
- You can increase your money, without risk, in government or corporate bonds.
- You can use the RRSP rules to sell yourself assets that you own, and get a tax break for doing so.
- You can invest in a mutual fund, have it pay the interest on money borrowed to make the investment, and then write that interest off your taxable income.
- You can invest for growth without risk in segregated funds.
- You can use an RRSP to increase the down payment on a first home.
- And you can get wise and reputable financial advice for free.

With these things possible, why are most middle-class Canadians slipping behind financially? It can only be because they're not aware of what a powerful time we live in for increasing personal assets. Money is cheap. Financial markets are soaring. Inflation is virtually gone. And the surge into mutual funds, equities, and government securities by millions of people in the year 2000—now just months away—will make those who see it coming and who take action, secure and comfortable.

AN AFFORDABLE NEWSLETTER OF TAX AND INVESTMENT STRATEGIES

The Turner Report is a newsletter you can receive 10 times a year. Its intention is clear: to present current strategies for reducing your tax exposure and investment opportunities that make sense. It covers mutual funds, strip bonds, seg funds, real estate, precious metals, stocks, oil and gas, and all aspects of personal finance that you need to know about.

The Turner Report does not suffer from the long lead times that books demand, nor is it another Bay Street publication written by a committee. Of course, it has nothing to sell. Instead, it's the living extension of this book, my financial guide for baby boomers, *2020: New Rules for the New Age*, *The Defence*, *2015: After the Boom,* and *The Strategy*. It is as timely and inexpensive as I can possibly make it.

In every issue:

- A national panel of top financial advisers gives expert advice to individual subscribers.
- Product Showcase offers an inside look at some of the hottest mutual funds available, and their performance.
- Features on the best tax and investment strategies.
- My personal analysis of current economic and market events, and predictions of where we are headed.
- Special offers to subscribers, including advance ordering of my books before they are available anywhere else.

The cost is less than $5 an issue. And I will send you the first issue as a gift for subscribing. If you are not satisfied, send it back for a full refund. No risk.

Of course, there are many good investment newsletters currently available. But if I thought any one of them was adequate for aggressive middle-class Canadians, aged 30 to 65, who are determined to succeed, then I would simply recommend it instead of writing my own.

But to date, I haven't found one that combines tax and investment strategies in the big-picture context of where the economy is headed or the impact that demographics will have. Nobody seems to be showing people how to get ahead at a time with frozen salaries, job insecurity, volatile markets, and rising taxes.

There are ways. Powerful ones. And now, more than ever, the difference between financial independence and dependence has come down to one thing, and one thing only: knowledge.

Appendix

PERSONAL INCOME TAX TABLES

The tax tables here are for taxable, not gross, income, and do not reflect any clawbacks, while assuming EI, CPP or QPP premiums are paid.

1999 PERSONAL INCOME TAX RATES (%)

Combined federal and provincial

Source: KPMG

1999 taxable income	$6,750– 29,590	$29,591– 35,400	$35,401– 39,000	$39,001– 59,180	$59,181– 63,392	$63,393– & over
British Columbia (1)						
Salary	24.8	38.9	38.9	38.9/49.0	49.5	49.5/52.3
Interest	26.4	40.3	40.3	40.3/44.4	49.5	50.9/54.2
Dividends	7.1	24.5	24.5	24.5/27.0	33.4	34.4/36.6
Capital Gains	19.8	30.2	30.2	30.2/33.3	37.1	38.2/40.6
Alberta (2)						
Salary	25.0	37.9	37.9	37.9/40.1	44.6	45.2
Interest	25.8	39.1	39.1	39.1/40.1	44.6	45.6
Dividends	7.4	24.1	24.1	24.1/24.7	30.4	31.1
Capital Gains	19.3	29.3	29.3	29.3/30.0	33.5	34.2
Saskatchewan (3)						
Salary	28.2	41.9	41.9	43.8/45.3	50.7	50.8
Interest	29.1	43.3	43.3	43.3/45.5	50.5	51.6

1999 PERSONAL INCOME TAX RATES (%) continued

Combined federal and provincial

Dividends	10.0	27.8	27.8	27.8/29.3	35.5	36.3
Capital Gains	21.8	32.5	32.5	32.5/34.2	37.9	38.7
Manitoba (4)						
Salary	27.2	40.6/42.6	42.6	42.6/43.9	48.4	49.0
Interest	28.4	42.3/44.3	44.3	44.3	49.0	50.1
Dividends	9.6	27.0/29.5	29.5	29.5	35.4	36.1
Capital Gains	21.3	31.7/33.2	33.2	33.2	36.7	37.6
Ontario (5)						
Salary	23.7	36.3	36.3	36.3/44.1	44.1/48.6	48.8
Interest	27.0	41.3	41.3	41.3/44.3	49.4	50.8/50.3
Dividends	7.3	25.2	25.2	25.2/27.0	33.3	34.3/33.9
Capital Gains	20.3	31.0	31.0	31.0/33.2	37.0	38.1/37.2
New Brunswick (6)						
Salary	27.2	41.6	41.6	47.7	48.2	48.3/49.7
Interest	28.4	43.4	43.4	43.4	48.4	69.9/50.4
Dividends	7.7	26.4	26.4	32.7	32.7	33.7/34.0
Capital Gains	21.3	32.6	32.6	32.6	36.3	37.4/37.8

Nova Scotia (7)						
Salary	26.8	41.0	41.0	42.1	47.0/47.4	47.4/49.2
Interest	27.6	42.3	42.3	42.3	47.1	48.6/49.7
Dividends	7.5	25.7	25.7	25.7	31.8	32.8/33.5
Capital Gains	20.7	31.7	31.7	31.7	35.3	36.4/37.2
Prince Edward Island (8)						
Salary	27.0	41.2	41.2	41.2/44.0	49.0/49.4	49.5
Interest	27.6	42.3	42.3	42.3	47.1	48.6/50.3
Dividends	7.5	25.7	25.7	25.7	31.8	32.8/34.0
Capital Gains	20.7	31.7	31.7	31.7	35.3	36.4/37.7
Newfoundland (9)						
Salary	28.7	43.9	43.9	43.9/52.3	52.3/52.8	52.9
Interest	29.2	44.7	44.7	44.7/46.5	51.9	53.3
Dividends	7.9	27.2	27.2	27.2/28.3	35.0	36.0
Capital Gains	21.9	33.5	33.5	33.5/34.9	38.9	40.0
Yukon (10)						
Salary	24.0	37.5	37.1	39.0/40.2	44.8/45.5	46.1
Interest	26.0	39.8	39.8	39.8	44.4/45.1	46.6
Dividends	7.0	24.2	24.2	24.2	30.0/31.0	31.4
Capital Gains	19.5	29.8	29.8	29.8	33.3/33.8	34.9

1999 PERSONAL INCOME TAX RATES (%) continued

Combined federal and provincial

Northwest Territories (10)						
Salary	23.2	36.2	37.1	37.7/38.9	43.4	43.9
Interest	25.2	38.5	38.5	38.5	42.9	44.4
Dividends	6.8	23.5	23.4	23.4	29.0	30.0
Capital Gains	18.9	28.9	28.9	28.9	32.2	33.3

Secondary rate thresholds by province:

1. $55,000 and $79,410 for salary, $53,664 and $78,208 for investment income.
2. $45,384 for salary and $44,050 for investment income.
3. $40,360 for salary and $39,205 for investment income.
4. $30,000.
5. $52,269 and $67,300 for salary, $50,937 and $66,108 for investment income.
6. $93,024 for salary and $91,830 for investment income.
7. $78,241 for salary and $77,043 for investment income.
8. $92,731 for salary and $91,532 for investment income.
9. $59,770 for salary and $58,500 for investment income.
10. $61,666 for salary and $60,469 for investment income.

1999 PERSONAL INCOME TAX RATES (%)

continued

Combined federal and provincial rates for Quebec

On Salary

Taxable Income	Rate
$6,750–8,780	13.9
$8,781–14,000	32.1
$14,001–23,000	34.3
$23,001–29,590	37.3
$29,591–32,535	44.8
$32,536–35,400	44.8
$35,401–39,000	44.8
$39,001–50,000	44.8/49.0
$50,001–54,395	48.2
$54,396–59,180	49.0
$59,181–63,400	51.6
$63,401 and over	51.6/52.2

On Investment Income

Taxable Income	Interest	Dividends	Capital Gains
$6,459–8,349	14.7	4.0	11.0
$8,350–14,000	34.1	16.9	25.6
$14,001–23,000	36.1	19.4	27.1
$23,001–29,590	38.2	22.0	28.6
$29,591–31,000	46.0	31.7	34.5
$31,001–50,000	47.1	32.6	35.3
$50,001–52,625	48.2	34.0	36.1
$52,626–59,180	48.9	34.5	36.7
$59,181–62,195	51.5	37.7	38.6
$62,196 and over	52.6	39.4	39.5

Index